TOUGH ENOUGH

MENTAL TOUGHNESS TRAINING FOR BOXING AND COMBAT SPORTS

Sammy Franco

Also by Sammy Franco

Speed Boxing Secrets
Heavy Bag Training
Heavy Bag Combinations
Heavy Bag Workout
The Heavy Bag Bible
Double End Bag Training
The Complete Body Opponent Bag Book
Cane Fighting
The Widow Maker Compendium
Invincible: Mental Toughness Techniques for Peak Performance
Unleash Hell: A Step-by-Step Guide to Devastating Widow Maker Combinations
Feral Fighting: Advanced Widow Maker Fighting Techniques
The Widow Maker Program: Extreme Self-Defense for Deadly Force Situations
Savage Street Fighting: Tactical Savagery as a Last Resort
Stand and Deliver: A Street Warrior's Guide to Tactical Combat Stances
Maximum Damage: Hidden Secrets Behind Brutal Fighting Combinations
First Strike: End a Fight in Ten Seconds or Less!
The Bigger They Are, The Harder They Fall
Self-Defense Tips and Tricks
Kubotan Power: Quick & Simple Steps to Mastering the Kubotan Keychain
Gun Safety: For Home Defense and Concealed Carry
Out of the Cage: A Guide to Beating a Mixed Martial Artist on the Street
Warrior Wisdom: Inspiring Ideas from the World's Greatest Warriors
War Machine: How to Transform Yourself Into a Vicious and Deadly Street Fighter
1001 Street Fighting Secrets
When Seconds Count: Self-Defense for the Real World
Killer Instinct: Unarmed Combat for Street Survival
Street Lethal: Unarmed Urban Combat

Tough Enough
Copyright © 2018 by Sammy Franco
ISBN: 978-1-941845-62-2
Printed in the United States of America

Published by Contemporary Fighting Arts, LLC.
Visit us Online at: **ContemporaryFightingArts.com**

All rights reserved. Except for use in a review, no portion of this book may be reproduced in any form without the express written permission of the author. Direct inquiries and/or orders to the above address.

For author interviews or publicity information, please send inquiries in care of the publisher.

Contents

What This Book Can Do For You	VII
Chapter 1: Mental Toughness for Combat Sports	1
Chapter 2: The Mental Toughness Package	17
Chapter 3: Steps to Mental Toughness	49
Chapter 4: Physical Training for Mental Toughness	57
Chapter 5: Mental Training for Mental Toughness	99
Chapter 6: Mental Toughness Programs	121
Appendix	135
Glossary	147
About Sammy Franco	177

"We don't rise to the level of our expectations, we fall to the level of our training."

- Archilochus

Disclaimer!

The author, publisher, and distributors of this book disclaim any liability from loss, injury, or damage, personal or otherwise, resulting from the information and procedures in this book. This book is for academic study only.

The information contained in this book is not designed to diagnose, treat, or manage any physical health conditions.

Before you begin any exercise or activity, including those suggested in this book, it is important to check with your physician to see if you have any condition that might be aggravated by strenuous training.

What This Book Can Do For You!

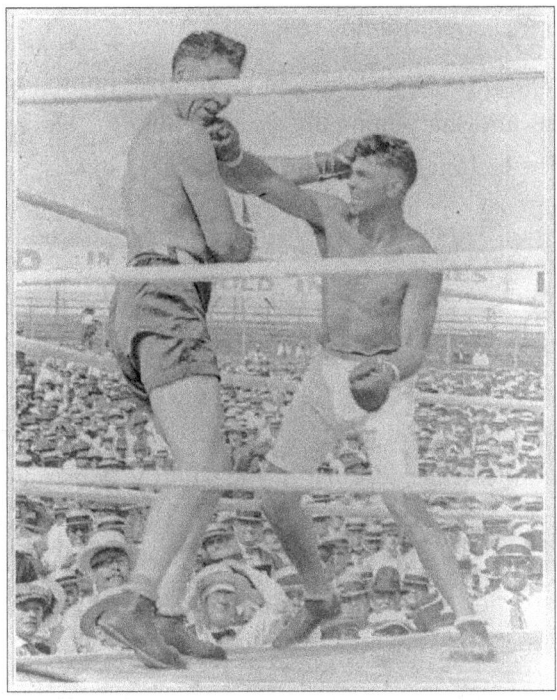

Tough Enough contains time-tested techniques, drills and strategies for improving mental toughness in combat sports like boxing and mixed martial arts. Besides sports performance, it also teaches you how to unlock the true power of your mind and achieve success in high-risk professions, self-defense, fitness, and other peak performance activities.

However, you don't have to be a professional boxer or mixed martial arts competitor to benefit from my unique mental toughness book. In fact, the mental skills featured in this indispensable program can be used by anyone who wants to reach their full potential.

Unlike other mental toughness books, Tough Enough doesn't

bog you down with boring theories, mind-numbing case studies, and confusing language. Instead, it's written in simple terms that you can easily understand so you can quickly put these mental toughness skills into your current training regimen.

Tough Enough contains new and innovative training methods for developing and sharpening the essential building blocks of mental toughness. The techniques and exercises featured in this book are based on my 30+ years of research, training and teaching the fighting sciences. They have helped thousands of my students excel and achieve their personal goals, and I'm confident they will help you reach new levels of success.

In this comprehensive book, you'll find step-by-step strategies for dealing with the debilitating fear and anxiety often associated with fighting. In essence, it provides you with the mental body armor necessary to cope, perform and prevail in all types of combat sports. By studying and practicing the concepts and principles in this book, you will feel a renewed sense of empowerment, enabling you to dominate your opponent and excel in your sport.

Tough Enough has seven chapters, each one covers a critical aspect of mental toughness. In addition, I have included a glossary of terms and appendix. Since this is both a skill-building workbook and mental training guide, feel free to write in the margins, underline passages, and dog-ear the pages.

Finally, I encourage you to read this book from beginning to end, chapter by chapter. Only after you have read the entire book should you treat it as a reference and skip around, reading those chapters or topics that directly apply to you.

Good luck with your training and your goals!

Sammy Franco
ContemporaryFightingArts.com

Chapter One
Mental Toughness for Combat Sports

Tough Enough

Chapter 1: Mental Toughness for Combat Sports

What is Mental Toughness?

Mental toughness is a performance mechanism utilizing a collection of mental qualities that allows a person to cope, perform and prevail through the stress of extreme adversity.

Mental toughness is also a form of self-mastery that plays an essential role in determining optimal performance and success in combat, sports, health, and other important aspects of life. Like any skill or attribute, mental toughness is something that can be learned and developed.

Unfortunately, many people use the term "mental toughness" loosely. Some self-appointed experts claim that it's simply a collection of positive qualities that help a person cope with a tough situation.

For example, this might include something as trivial as preparing for a midterm exam or working in a competitive business environment. Unfortunately, such a cavalier interpretation is misleading and weakens the very essence of this vital performance mechanism.

Finally, not every form of mental toughness is alike. For instance, the mental resilience necessary to survive a prisoner-of-war camp is dramatically different from than the mental strength required to endure and complete the Marathon des Sables. While the two might share similar mental toughness attributes, they are drastically

Tough Enough

different experiences, requiring dissimilar forms of performance training.

The 6 Elements of Extreme Adversity

Genuine mental toughness is demonstrated when you are confronted with extreme forms of adversity. Examples would include, fighting a superior opponent in the ring or performing a mission critical task in a hostile and dangerous environment. Generally, extreme adversity will include most of the following six elements:

- A degree of Danger
- The element of Risk
- The presence of Fear
- The possibility of Loss
- A challenge to your Self-confidence
- The experience of Pain (emotional or physical)

In fact, genuine mental strength requires you to activate every fiber of your being (mentally, emotionally, physically, and spiritually). It's no wonder mental toughness is readily identified with elite military units, like the United States Navy SEALs. These elite warriors are the foundation of Naval Special Warfare combat forces. They are considered the best of the best because they are trained to

Pictured here, a Navy Special Warfare Trident insignia worn exclusively by U.S. Navy SEALs.

Chapter 1: Mental Toughness for Combat Sports

conduct a wide range of Special Operations missions in all types of extreme climates and hostile environments, including the sea, air, and land.

Physical and Psychological Adversity

Extreme adversity can materialize in one of two forms: physical or psychological. Physical adversity requires you to cope and perform during a physically stressful event or circumstance. For example, physical adversity can be a brutal boxing match with a formidable opponent. Or, it could be something less menacing like a competitive wrestling match against a powerful and determined opponent. Both of these examples, however, will still require a substantial amount of mental toughness to cope and perform under these taxing circumstances.

Conversely, psychological adversity requires you to cope and perform during a psychologically stressful event or circumstance. For example, it might require you to withstand the psychological torment of a bully or the relentless taunting of a drill sergeant.

Many occupations might also expose you to various forms of psychological adversity. For example, consider a police officer who must confront and diffuse a verbally abusive crowd or a professional athlete who is regularly insulted by overzealous spectators.

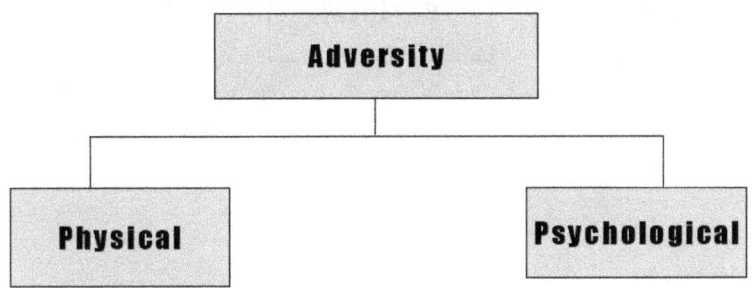

Adversity can be divided into two separate categories: physical and psychological.

Tough Enough

Both of these examples require a certain degree of mental toughness to cope and perform when faced with the stress of adversity. Finally, physical and psychological adversity are not mutually exclusive. More often than not, they are experienced at the same time.

3 Objectives of Mental Toughness for Combat Sports

In the world of combat sports, mental toughness has three primary objectives. They include the following:

- To **cope** with adversity.
- To **perform** during adversity.
- To **prevail** from adversity.

The three primary objectives of mental toughness is to cope, perform and prevail in the face of adversity.

Chapter 1: Mental Toughness for Combat Sports

Coping with Adversity

Mental toughness requires you to accept adverse circumstances. This is counter-intuitive for most people because we are born with a natural instinct to avoid conflict and discomfort. In fact, we often make our situations worse by avoiding them. Therefore, the first step to coping with adversity is to identify and embrace it. Recognize it for what it is – a legitimate obstacle to your goal.

Effectively coping with adversity also means you must immediately manage and control the stress that comes with it. This is critical because it determines whether or not you'll be able to perform at the right moment.

Stress is simply the physiological and psychological arousal caused by a stressor. A stressor is any activity, situation, circumstance, event, experience, or condition that causes a person to experience either physical or mental anxiety. Stressors come in many different forms (mental, physical and emotional), and they can wreck havoc on anyone who is not prepared to handle them.

The first step to manage stress is to observe and acknowledge it. Next, you must immediately prohibit it from affecting your mind and body. You can accomplish this by using a wide range of coping skills, including meditation, mental visualization, positive self-talk, and controlled breathing techniques. Stress inoculation techniques can also be used to minimize stressful events (more will be discussed in a later chapter).

Finally, you must redirect your thoughts and actions to the performance stage of mental toughness. Keep in mind, these three steps are conducted and completed within seconds of identifying the stressor.

When performing in the face of adversity, your actions must fulfill three essential requirements: efficiency, effectiveness, and safety.

Boxing Performance in the Face of Adversity

Once you have confronted and accepted adversity and managed the stress associated with it, it's time to take action! Performing under the pressure of adversity will require that your course of action meet three essential requirements: efficiency, effectiveness, and safety.

- **Efficiency** – you course of action is performed in the quickest and most economical fashion.

Chapter 1: Mental Toughness for Combat Sports

- **Effectiveness** – your course of action achieves your goal or objective.

- **Safety** – you course of action is performed with the least possible amount of risk or danger.

Prevailing in the Face of Adversity

It's not enough to survive through adversity. For example, if you're a professional boxer engaged in a brutal match, your ultimate goal is to win or prevail. Similarly, if you are a soldier, your goal might entail defeating a hostile enemy in order to achieve the objectives of your mission. On the battlefield or in the boxing ring, your goal is plain and simple – beat your opponent and win!

Who Needs Mental Toughness?

Anyone can benefit from mental toughness. However, there are certain people who require it. In fact, mental toughness is an essential tool necessary for many occupations, professions, and activities.

Tough Enough

For example, take a look at America's favorite sport, football. It illustrates the vital necessity of mental toughness. Watch a game and you'll observe some interesting things, like the tremendous power and strength of a 280-pound lineman moving with the speed of a freight train in an all-out effort to crush the quarterback. Pain is exalted; I've heard of a player who continued a game after having torn off his fingertips. You can find other examples of mental toughness in boxing, mixed martial arts, hockey, rugby, etc.

Mental toughness, however, is not limited to sports. Consider, for example, a rookie police officer fresh out of the academy. There's a very good reason the trainee is accompanied by a field training officer (FTO) during his initial weeks on the job. Besides teaching and evaluating the rookie, the FTO serves as a role model, mentor, and coach who imparts the mental toughness skills necessary for officer survival.

Here is a brief list of fields that require mental toughness:

- **Boxing**
- **Mixed Martial Arts**
- **Martial Arts**
- **Military**
- **Law enforcement**
- **Self-defense**
- **Executive and personal protection**
- **Private security**
- **General Sports and athletics**
- **Fitness and Health**

Chapter 1: Mental Toughness for Combat Sports

Two Types of Mental Toughness

Mental toughness skills can be applied to a broad spectrum of circumstances and situations. However, it exists in varying degrees, ranging from mild to extreme. For example, the mental toughness attributes required for a professional boxer to win a match, will differ from the mental resilience needed to survive a bloody fire-fight in a war zone. While the two examples might share similar mental toughness qualities, their environment, training, objectives, and stressors will differ significantly.

Therefore, there are two broad categories of mental toughness that, in reality, differ in very significant ways: combative and competitive mental toughness.

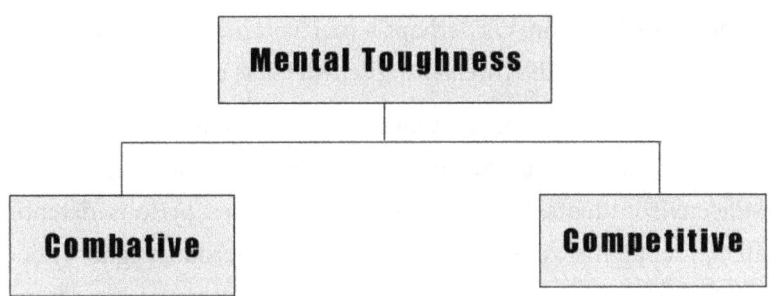

There are two general categories of mental toughness: combative and competitive.

Combative Mental Toughness

Combative mental toughness applies to professionals and individuals who must live or work in dangerous and hostile environments, where violence is a very real possibility. Moreover, their occupation requires them to perform high-risk duties while making critical decisions during life-and-death situations. Many of these individuals will face life-threatening encounters on a daily basis.

Tough Enough

Some include:

- **Military personnel**
- **Law Enforcement officer**
- **Self-Defense practitioner**
- **Security professional**
- **Doormen and Bouncer**
- **Bounty hunters**

Combative mental toughness is not limited to high-risk occupations. In fact, it's useful to anyone who must confront violence and aggression while risking the possibility of sustaining a severe injury or possible death. Take, for example, a law-abiding citizen who must use deadly force to protect himself and his family from a horrific home invasion. Or perhaps a martial artist who trains and prepares himself for life threatening self-defense encounters.

Finally, combative mental toughness serves as a cognitive survival mechanism for civilians who are forced to live in dangerous and hostile environments. Examples include war zones, prisons, detention centers, mental institutions, and extremely dangerous neighborhoods and districts.

Chapter 1: Mental Toughness for Combat Sports

Competitive Mental Toughness

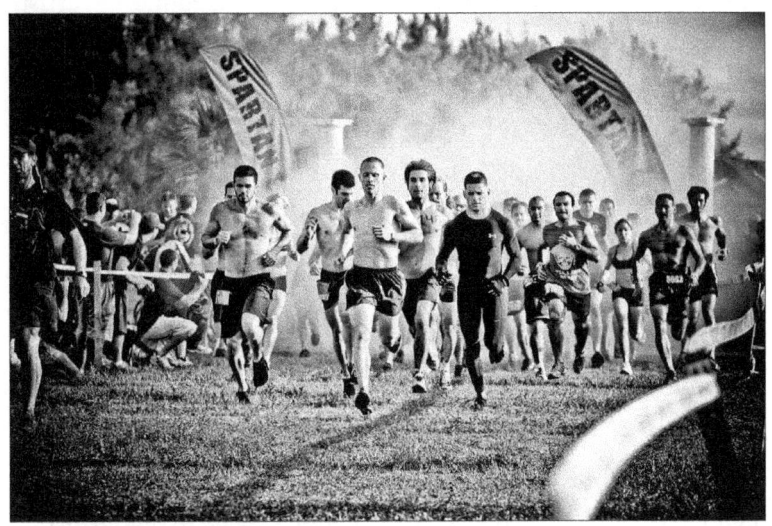

Mental toughness is not just for warriors. In fact, it can help anyone achieve both personal and professional success in our increasingly competitive world. I refer to this as competitive mental toughness. In essence, it permits you to push through the stress and pressure of adversity with the ultimate objective of achieving a personal goal.

Competitive mental toughness is a vital source of power for individuals who want to achieve personal peak performance in any activity or endeavor. This mindset plays a crucial role in determining optimal performance and success in such things as sports, fitness, health, and other important aspects of life. Unlike combat mental toughness, this form of mental strength doesn't entail danger or violence, nor does it require making critical life-and-death decisions.

In this respect, competitive mental toughness is ideal for anyone who wants to be capable of optimum performance while faced with challenging circumstances. Moreover, it can be readily used by anyone, regardless of skill level. For example, it might include high-profile professional athletes, entertainers, weekend warriors, gym rats, distance runners, triathletes, boxers, mixed martial artists, bodybuilders, etc.

Competitive mental toughness also provides additional benefits, including improved self-discipline and self-esteem, enhanced creativity, improved motivation, and a greater sense of autonomy. Finally, possessing this skill and ability to withstand great hardships will benefit anyone who doesn't want to be a slave to fear, apprehension, and self-doubt.

Mental Toughness for Sports

Mental toughness is essential to succeeding in all types of competitive sports. Regardless, if you are playing a team or individual sport, it provides the psychological edge to outperform your opponent.

Athletes who lack mental toughness will often "choke" and fall apart from the pressure of a competitive event. Some will get intimidated and psyched out by their opponent, while others abandon their focus and concentration, allowing their imaginations to run wild.

However, an athlete who possesses mental toughness doesn't suffer from these anxieties and problems. Instead, he employs the necessary coping skills to handle the stress and anxiety associated with sports competition. In fact, he views competition from a healthy and productive perspective that makes him remain relaxed under pressure. This state of mental relaxation permits him to enjoy the moment and perform at his peak.

When developed properly, competitive mental toughness provides the athlete with laser-like focus, confidence, and mental clarity to consistently achieve his or her personal goals. Finally, achieving greater levels of sports performance is not an easy task,

Chapter 1: Mental Toughness for Combat Sports

however mental toughness provides the necessary drive and motivation to compete against yourself and consistently break personal records.

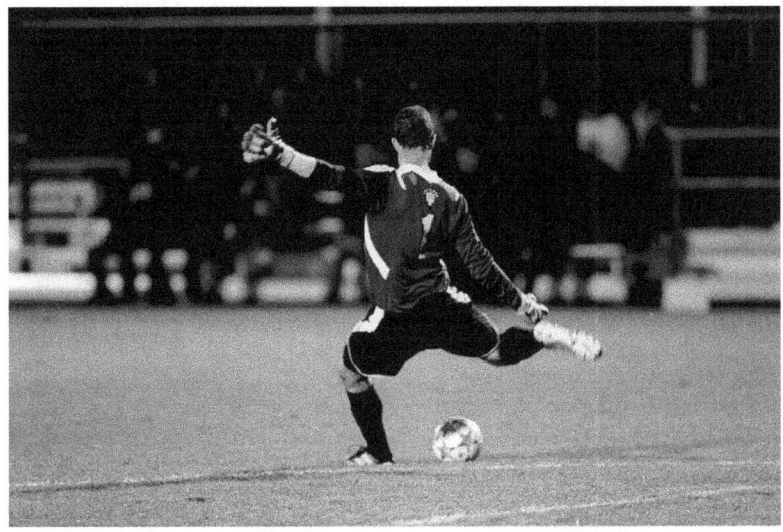

Mental toughness provides a tremendous competitive edge for athletes.

Mental Toughness for Fitness and Health

In sports, as well as many other physical performance activities, complacency often leads to mediocrity. To excel in all types of physical activities, you are required to practice and workout on a regular basis. Unfortunately, there will be mental and physical barriers that will sabotage your training.

For example, you might be going through a mental slump and simply don't feel like working out. Or perhaps, you might be working through a mild and annoying injury that makes you second guess your skills and abilities. You might be dealing with the discomfort of muscle soreness from a previous training session or experiencing family or relationship problems. All of these examples, as trivial as they might seem, can significantly diminish your progress.

Mental toughness, however, gives you the mental resilience to push through these barriers and stay on track with your training regimen. It engenders a vital discipline that allows you to push through discomfort and distractions so that you can complete your workout session.

Getting Motivated and Determined

Just about everyone will agree that sticking to a fitness, diet or health program is hard work. In fact, most people fail to achieve their personal goals because they lack the determination and motivation to stay on course.

Failure to achieve personal goals is a result of poor motivation and willpower. However, mental toughness skills will strengthen your mind, making you more motivated and determined to achieve your personal goals. Laziness and negativity are eliminated and replaced with positive energy and a desire and willingness to follow through with your intentions.

Chapter Two
The Mental Toughness Package

Tough Enough

Mental Toughness Attributes

Now that you have a general understanding of mental toughness, it's time to delve deeper into this invaluable source of mind power. Mental toughness consists of several interrelated elements know as attributes. Essentially, this collection of attributes can either be *reactive* or *proactive*.

A reactive attribute is a quality that allows you to cope and perform during the immediate stress and pressure of adversity. While a proactive attribute is used to maintain optimum performance under less stressful conditions. Both types of attributes serve as the essential building blocks of mental toughness.

The Mental Toughness Package

During my 30+ years of teaching the fighting sciences to law enforcement, military personnel, athletes and people of all backgrounds, I have discovered that a complete mental toughness package consists of the following core attributes.

- Instrumental Aggression
- Assertiveness
- Resilience
- Self-Confidence
- Self-Discipline
- Awareness
- Attention Control
- Philosophical Resolution
- Responsibility
- Courage

What About the Killer Instinct?

Please don't confuse mental toughness with its cousin the killer instinct. While both have similar attributes, mental toughness is the stable internal climate that nourishes and ultimately brings about the killer instinct. The killer instinct is an emotionless, primal mindset that surges to your conscious mind and transforms you into a vicious combatant. Deep within every person is a deadly primal power, a virtuous killer instinct that is cold, calculated, and primed for destruction. The killer instinct is also a reservoir of energy and strength. It can channel your destructiveness by producing a mental wellspring of cold, destructive energy. If necessary, it fuels the determination to battle until the very end.

Nature or Nurture

Are mental toughness attributes learned or instinctual? This question has perplexed psychologists and coaches for decades, creating a debate over the nature theory and the nurture theory.

Chapter 2: The Mental Toughness Package

Advocates of the nature theory believe that mental toughness is innately linked to biological, genetic and physiological factors. Built into the machine if you will. On the other hand, advocates of the nurture theory believe that mental toughness is learned from your environment and various other external factors.

The debate between these two schools of thought has gone on for some time and will most likely continue. I strongly believe that mental toughness is a combination of both nature and nurture. The raw instinct for mental toughness was manifested from the beginning of man's existence. It was a vital factor in his survival against nature's brutality, including the threat of other aggressors like himself. His adaption to adversity, accompanied with his unique problem solving abilities seem to be a combination of both genetic factors and environmental influences. Where one influence leaves off and the other picks up is impossible to say.

However, the important point is that mental toughness can be learned and developed. The first step, however, is to recognize and understand its core attributes. Only then can mental toughness be fully developed, and ultimately honed to maximize your performance during critical situations.

Now, let's take a closer look at the individual components of mental toughness. We will start with Instrumental aggression.

Instrumental Aggression

For many people, the concept of aggression immediately conjures up images of senseless and overt acts of violence directed against another individual. There are others who believe that human aggression is the root of all evil and the primary cause of social conflict and global warfare.

However, human aggression is a necessary behavior trait that has ensured the survival of our species, and it's also a vital component of mental toughness. Essentially, there are two distinct categories of aggression: instrumental and reactive.

Instrumental aggression – purposeful and controlled aggressive action designed to help achieve a particular objective or goal. A boxer executing a punishing combination attack on his opponent, or a mixed martial artists performing a brutal ground and pound, are good examples.

Reactive aggression – impulsive and emotionally charged aggressive action that is provoked by an external source. For example, a professional athlete who engages in a road rage incident is a good example of reactive aggression.

Mental toughness regularly requires the application of instrumental aggression. As a matter of fact, I define instrumental aggression as purposeful and controlled violence directed to a specific person while maintaining both strategic and tactical objectives.

Instrumental aggression is particularly important for occupations and activities that require you to administer physical force, such as military service, police work, private security, and self-defense. Full-contact sports like boxing, mixed martial arts, kickboxing, wrestling, football, rugby, lacrosse, roller derby, and ice hockey will also benefit from controlled aggression.

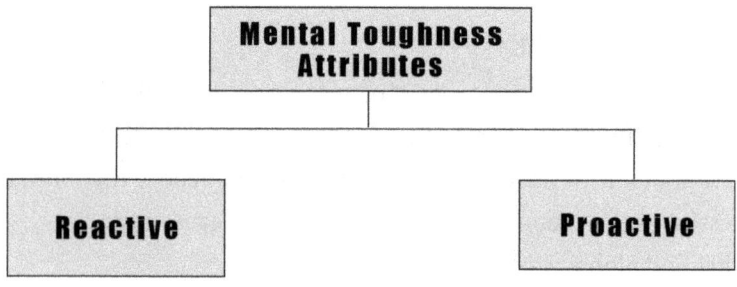

There are two different types of attributes that comprise mental toughness: Reactive and Proactive

Chapter 2: The Mental Toughness Package

Assertiveness

Just about every sporting event or high-risk occupation involves some form of interaction and communication between people. For example, in sports there will be an exchange of words or behaviors between opponents, teammates, coaches, family members, and spectators. In high-risk occupations like police work, you might be required to interact with a host of different people including supervisors, co-workers, civilians, and criminals.

In order to perform at your best, you must possess a healthy degree of assertiveness. Assertiveness is a form of behavior characterized as a confident and positive expression of your thoughts, feeling, and needs. On the other hand, it doesn't mean being pushy, intrusive, confrontational, or autocratic.

Highly competitive sporting events are not won by meek individuals. Athletes must possess healthy communication skills. They must be able to express their goals, needs and rights to other teammates and coaches. Failing to assert yourself with both teammates and coaches can be problematic and self-destructive. Actively avoiding unpleasant confrontations or suppressing or denying your feelings can be damaging on many levels, resulting in loss of confidence and self-respect. In addition, you might experience feelings of powerlessness, anger, frustration, anxiousness, and resentment. More importantly, passive communication tells others that you are weak and not to be taken seriously.

Resilience

Resilience is the ability to recover quickly from various forms of adversity. Essentially, it provides the mental strength to "bounce back" or "get back on your feet" and continue pursuing your goal or objective. For example, an athlete might sustain a physical injury or embarrassing performance mistake. A soldier might experience

Tough Enough

psychological trauma from war, or a police officer might experience post-traumatic stress from a deadly shootout with the criminal. As diverse as these examples might be, all of them require a substantial amount of mental resiliency to recover and get back on track.

Resiliency requires you to be adaptable. You must possess the necessary physical and mental skills to adapt to the rapidly changing circumstances of your environment. In combat, for example, factors and circumstances change like the wind. A prepared combatant knows how and when to adapt to his environment. Adaptability allows one to adjust to new or different conditions or circumstances both physically and psychologically. In the heat of a fight, a fighter doesn't have the luxury of questioning change. He or she cannot overly scrutinize a particular situation. In fact, he must simply conform to the immediate demands of his predicament.

Two Types of Resilience

There are two distinct categories of mental resiliency: **Immediate** and **Reflective**. Let's take a look at each one.

Immediate Resilience

Immediate resilience requires you to adapt immediately to the stress you experience during a crisis or event. For example, consider a professional boxer who encounters an unexpected hook to the head during a match. To stay on his feet and avoid going "down for the count", he must immediately adapt and make the necessary adjustments to regain his equilibrium, balance, and mental composure. During his opponent's flurry of punches that follow suit, the boxer must remain focused and not fold under pressure. It's during this crisis moment, he must demonstrate the immediate resilience to bounce back and endure the pain and emotional anxiety associated with his opponent's vicious assault.

Immediate resilience is particularly important for grueling endurance sports like triathlons, marathons, ultramarathons, and extreme obstacle races. Endurance sports are about mental willpower. They require you to compete against your most formidable opponent – yourself. In order to perform well, you must possess the mental resilience to cope with the inevitable pain, fatigue, and exhaustion that comes with these types of endurance events. Immediate resilience simply gives you the mental wherewithal to push through these obstacles and win.

Reflective Resilience

Reflective resilience, on the other hand is the ability to bounce back from setbacks that involve either physical injury or mental trauma. In many ways, it's a form of picking up the pieces and rebounding from adversity. For example, a professional athlete who experiences a serious sports injury might become disheartened and question whether he has the skill and talent to pursue his journey. His despair brings him to a mental crossroad where he must summon the resilience to fight his fears and apprehensions. Reflective resilience provides the athlete with the strength and resolve to work his way back to his previous healthy state. Moreover, with serious thought and honest reflection, the athlete acquires a renewed sense of motivation and commitment.

Finally, reflective resilience is essential for individuals who experience psychological trauma from hazardous duties. Consider a soldier, who experiences the horrors of war might suffer from combat stress reaction (CSR) or a police officer who experiences a traumatic incident might develop post-traumatic stress. Reflective resilience acts as a type of mental armor that protects your psyche and helps you recover from a traumatic event.

Self-Confidence

Successful athletes thrive during high-pressure competition because they are confident they possess the skills and ability necessary to beat their opponents. Their self-confidence serves as an effective coping mechanism to overcome anxiety, self-doubt, intimidation, and fear during a high-performance event.

Self-confidence means having an unshakable trust in both your judgment skills and abilities. However, it should not be confused with arrogance or false bravado. In fact, you must be self-aware. You must have an accurate and realistic perspective of yourself including both your inherent strengths and weaknesses. When all is said and done, dangerous poisons like egotism, conceit and narcissism will undermine your goals by instilling a false reality.

Self-confidence can be infectious and will often have a spillover effect in team sports. For example, an athlete who believes in himself resolutely, often inspires his teammates to push past their limits during difficult circumstances. He might also energize spectators and fans to rally and cheer his team to victory. Conversely, players demonstrating low self-esteem, poor self-image and a lack of confidence can also cripple a team and bring it down to its collective knees.

Self-Discipline

Self-discipline is considered the single most important trait required to achieve personal excellence. As a matter of fact, it's self-discipline that separates the novice from the expert and the highly accomplished person from the underachiever. Self-discipline is the ability to work methodically and consistently toward a personal goal until it is achieved. In some instances, it might require you to work tirelessly day after day, week after week, and month after month until your objective is actualized.

Chapter 2: The Mental Toughness Package

Self-discipline requires you to control and manage your impulses, emotions and desires so you can effectively pursue and ultimately reach your goals. It means having the self-control to ignore the deleterious temptations of instant gratification, in favor of acquiring a more meaningful and sometimes arduous goal.

Self-discipline does not mean living your life like an ascetic monk or denying yourself worldly pleasures. It doesn't mean limiting or restricting your lifestyle or abstaining from enjoyable things. Rather, self-discipline means focusing your mind exclusively on a goal and directing all of your energy until you achieve your objective.

Self-discipline also means controlling your mind and body with positive and purposeful choices, instead of negative emotions, bad habits, and external influences. Simply put, self-discipline allows you to achieve your goals in a very efficient and effective manner.

The Three Steps of Self-Discipline

Self-discipline is not just a trait, it's also a skill that can be learned. It requires you to take three simple yet effective steps. First, you must make a specific decision. Second, you must take the necessary action for that decision. Third, you must follow-through with the proper course of action (despite the obstacles that come with it) until you achieve your goal or objective.

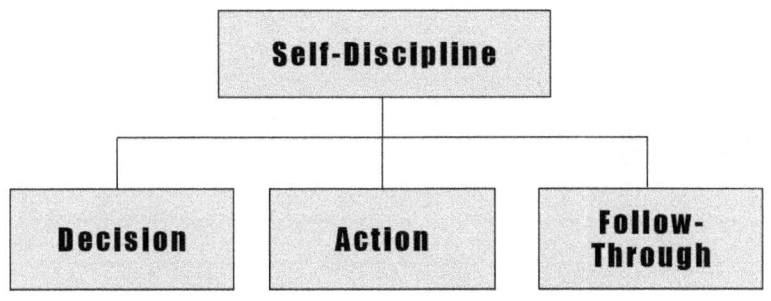

Self-discipline is a relatively simple three stage process.

Other Benefits of Self-Discipline

There are many other benefits of self-discipline, here are a few.

- Self-discipline increases your self-confidence.
- Self-discipline improves your creativity and imagination.
- Self-discipline sharpens and refines analytical thinking.
- Self discipline promotes leadership skills.
- Self-discipline generates respect from other people.
- Self-discipline gives you a greater passion for life.

Self-Discipline Exercises:

1. In your own words, briefly describe what self-discipline means to you.

_____
_____
_____
_____
_____
_____
_____
_____
_____

2. Describe the most self-disciplined athlete you know and explain his or her success.

_____
_____
_____
_____

Chapter 2: The Mental Toughness Package

_____
_____
_____
_____
_____

3. Describe the least self-disciplined person you know and explain his or her failures.

_____
_____
_____
_____
_____
_____
_____
_____

4. Name three aspects of your life that are in desperate need of self-discipline.

_____
_____
_____
_____
_____
_____
_____
_____

Tough Enough

5. Briefly describe three problems you are currently experiencing due to a lack of self-discipline.

_____
_____
_____
_____
_____
_____
_____
_____

6. Describe several benefits you will acquire from developing self-discipline.

_____
_____
_____
_____
_____
_____
_____
_____

Awareness

Your awareness or perception of people, places, actions, and objects is a vital component of mental toughness. In fact, peak performance in every activity or endeavor can only be achieved through the proper awareness skills. Awareness gives you the ability to respond rapidly and successfully to a wide variety of stressful situations and circumstances. In addition, it offers the necessary introspection to identify which aspects of yourself create obstacles that prevent you from achieving your goals.

Your Perception Matters

Awareness is directly linked to your perceptions. Perception is the interpretation of information acquired through one's senses when faced with a stressful or dangerous situation. You gather information through your five senses. Your eyes, ears, nose, and senses of touch and taste will provide a wealth of vital information about your environment. With adequate training, your senses can be sharpened, and your powers of observation enhanced.

The ability to process information varies from person to person. In fact, two people who witness the same event are likely to report it differently. This is referred to as "individual perception." In part, previous experiences can determine the manner in which a person will interpret stimuli. When it comes to achieving peak performance in combat and athletics, you must attempt to remove preconceived notions, assumptions, and biases that may lead to dangerously incorrect conclusions or oversights. These false reactions form barriers to your ability to grasp reality.

Two Types of Awareness

There are two types of awareness that are directly linked to mental toughness. They are: *situational* and *self-awareness*. Let's start by taking a look at situational awareness.

Situational Awareness

Situational awareness is total alertness, presence, and focus on virtually everything in your immediate surroundings. For example, if you are a soldier, police officer or security agent, you must train your senses to detect and assess the people, places, objects, and actions

Tough Enough

that can pose a danger to you. Do not think of situational awareness simply in terms of the five customary senses of sight, sound, smell, taste, and touch. In addition, the very real powers of instinct and intuition must also be developed and eventually relied upon.

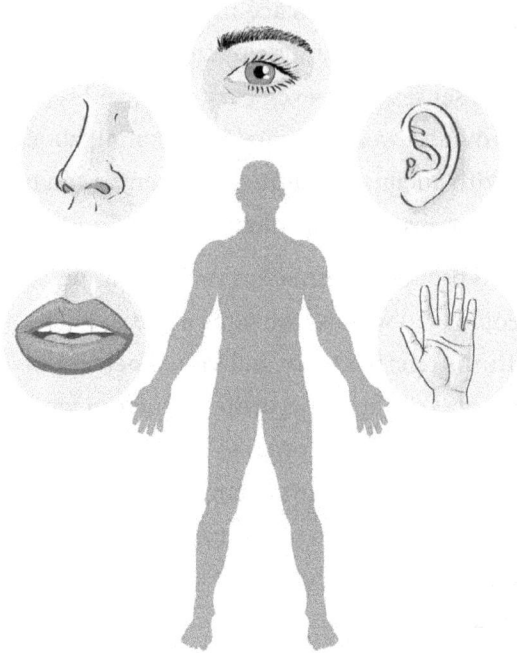

With proper training, your senses can be sharpened, and your powers of observation enhanced.

Self-defense clearly illustrates this point. For example, a vagrant congregating by your car, the stranger lingering in your apartment hallway, two men following you in a deserted parking lot, the stray dog ambling toward you in the park, a large limb hanging precariously from a tree… these are all obvious examples of persons, places, and objects that pose a threat to you.

Situational awareness also diminishes the potency of the criminal's favorite weapon – the element of surprise. Your ability to foresee and detect danger will diminish his ability to stalk you, or lie in wait in ambush zones. In addition to enhancing your ability to detect, avoid, and strategically neutralize ambush zones, situational awareness allows you to detect and avoid threats and dangers not necessarily predicated on the element of surprise. Some situations afford potential victims the luxury of seeing trouble coming. Nonetheless, it's remarkable how many people fail to heed obvious signs of danger because of poor awareness skills. They overlook the signals – belligerence, furtiveness, hostility, restlessness – so often manifested by criminal attackers. They neglect the opportunity to cross the street long before the shoulder-to-shoulder encounter with a pack of young toughs moving up the sidewalk. Once it's too late to avoid the confrontation, a whole new range of principles comes quickly into play.

How to Sharpen your Senses

Your five senses (sight, smell, touch, sound, and taste) can be sharpened through a variety of exercises designed to develop both raw detection and learned identification abilities.

For example, sit on a park bench for a given period of time and catalog the various objects and actions your five senses detect, then list the possible sources of the sensory data. With sufficient practice, you will make significant progress from being unable to detect a particular sound or smell to not only detecting it quickly and accurately, but also identifying its source. Remember that sensory development increases as these exercises are performed in different environmental settings.

Trust Your Instincts

Situational awareness also means trusting your instincts. Learn to rely on your innate ability to know or sense something without the use of rational thought. In many circumstances, immediate cognition will provide you with the necessary time to respond to a challenging or threatening situation. In some situations, going with your "gut" reaction can be just what is called for. Remember, when something doesn't seem right, or the objective data doesn't add up, then chances are something is wrong.

Self-Awareness

Self-awareness has been the subject of philosophers and mystics for centuries. Socrates said, "Know thyself." He believed self-knowledge to be essential to the attainment of true virtue. Self-awareness empowers athletes by giving them invaluable information about their strengths, weaknesses, attitudes, motivations, and beliefs.

The key to making positive changes in your behavior and ultimately improving your performance is first to understand yourself in relation to your sport. Self-awareness gives both athletes and warriors the experiential knowledge to control his or her performance during highly stressful events.

Self-awareness involves the harmonious integration of your mind and body to gain full-control of any high-pressure performance situation. It allows you to read, interpret, and understand what your body is telling you. As a result, you remain calm, focused, and in complete control of your emotions when experiencing both performance success and failures.

Moreover, self-awareness helps you mentally recall, imprint, and hopefully replicate the positive experiences of an ideal performance state. Conversely, it also helps you recognize, identify and avoid the negative and unproductive elements that come with a poor performance.

Different Forms of Combat Sports Performance

Awareness

- The fighter is focused exclusively on the immediate performance task.
- The fighter makes accurate assessments and adjustments during performance.
- The fighter recognizes his or her limitations while performing.
- The fighter understands the stressors that cause poor performance.
- The fighter is able to control his emotions during performance.

Self-Awareness Questions for Combat Sports Performance

The following questions were designed to start you thinking in the important process of self-awareness. Use them to form an overall personal profile of yourself.

1. What essential qualities do you bring to your sport?
2. What separates you from other athletes in your field?
3. What are your feelings (both positive and negative) about your sport?
4. What does performance success mean to you? Give examples.
5. What does performance failure mean to you? Give examples.
6. Exactly how do you feel when you perform at your best?
7. What enables you to perform at your best?
8. What contributes to your performance failures?

Tough Enough

9. Exactly how do you feel when you perform poorly?

Attention Control

Earlier, I discussed situational awareness and its importance for mental toughness. Situational awareness provides the raw data of your immediate surroundings, while attention control is the ability to select what stimuli to pay attention to and what to ignore. Attention control is actually a combination of two mental skills: selective attention and concentration.

Selective attention is the ability to filter out and ignore the unnecessary sights, sounds, sensations, thoughts, and emotions and focus exclusively on stimuli that is pertinent to your goal or objective. Simply put, it means selecting and discriminating the valuable data that is critically important to your task, from a considerable amount of junk. Concentration, on the other hand, is the ability to sustain attention over a specific period of time.

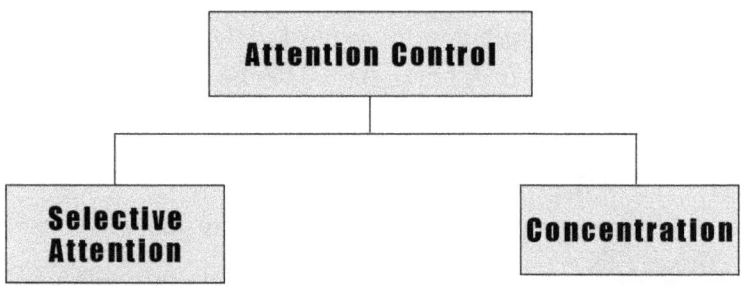

Attention control is a combination of both Selective Attention and Concentration.

Concentration Shifting

Both warriors and athletes are required to shift their attention constantly during critical performance moments. At any given time, they might be required to shift their focus from internal to external or broad to narrow. For example, during a professional fight, a mixed

Chapter 2: The Mental Toughness Package

martial artist must first focus his attention internally by develop a winning strategy predicated on his opponent's apparent strengths and weaknesses. Then, he shifts his attention to external factors like the opponent's range, movement, angle of attack, and punch trajectory. Finally, he narrows his focus even further by delivering a precisely timed knockout counter strike.

Two Sources of Distraction

Concentration requires a unified mind that is free from all types of distractions and fully focused on the immediate situation. Distractions are derived from one of two sources. The first is eternal, where in your mind wanders off or panics prior to or during a stressful situation.

The second is external when outside elements force your mind to lose focus. For example, when your opponent attempts to verbally "psych you out" for example. Or when you become physically injured during a dangerous crisis situation. Environmental conditions such as weather, lighting, terrain, and noise can also create external distractions.

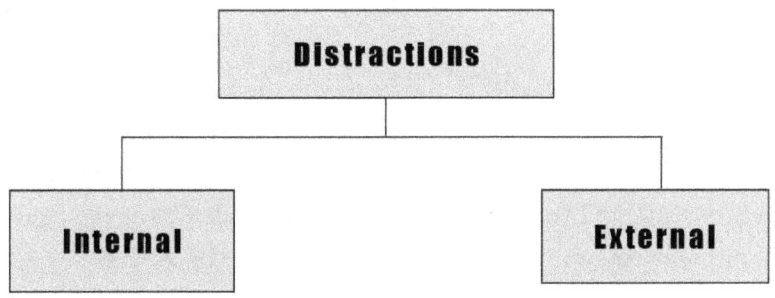

Distractions are derived from one of two source: Internal and External.

For this reason, I teach my students how to avoid being distracted by the opponent during the pre-contact stages of a self-defense altercation. For example, they are taught to disregard such things as psych-out techniques, threatening gestures, eye movements, abusive language, and drastic fluctuations in voice including tone, pitch, tempo, and volume.

Regardless of the source, distractions must be ignored and ultimately eliminated from your consciousness if you are to achieve peak performance in any endeavor.

Philosophical Resolution

Mental toughness requires you to address difficult and often controversial questions concerning the use of violence. Philosophical resolution of important martial issues contributes to a fighter's mental confidence and clarity. It is alarming to think of the many years spent by so many warriors achieving the capability to harm others, and even destroy life, with little or no time devoted to the intellectual resolution of questions concerning the ultimate use of violence.

Why are you reading this book? What is your greatest fear? What is the source of your spiritual strength, if any? What is the mind, and what does it mean to be conscious? What is the link between mental power and physical activity? Who are you? How do you know right from wrong?

These are only a few vital questions you must resolve honestly and fully before you can advance to the highest levels of combat awareness. If you haven't begun the quest to formulate the important questions and find your answers, then take a break. It's time to figure out just why you want to know the laws and skills of combat.

Responsibility

Responsibility is another core component of mental toughness. Essentially, it means being morally accountable for your own behavior. For example, athletes are responsible for their training and game performance as well as their relentless drive to improve themselves. They must consistently evaluate their performance and determine what must be done to eliminate mistakes in order to achieve peak performance. Consequently, they must take full responsibility for each and every decision and action they make during competition. They must take credit and responsibility for both victories and losses alike.

However, warriors and athletes are only responsible for what they control. Unnecessarily blaming yourself for things that are clearly out of your control is fruitless, and in many cases, self-destructive. The truth is you can still lose a game or battle, despite your best efforts.

The Pitfall of Excuses

Likewise, you must also avoid making excuses for performance failures that are clearly your responsibility. The bottom line is, you and only you must take responsibility for your mistakes and faults. If you make a mistake, own it and learn from it.

Excuses are false reasons or inaccurate justifications used to absolve you of responsibility. However, the truth is they are nothing more than unproductive lies designed to protect your ego. They are inherently dangerous to both the athlete and warrior because they distort reality and prevent the practitioner from learning from his or her mistake. Excuses contradict and undermine the self-awareness required to achieve all forms of peak performance. Therefore, it's in your best interest to consider adopting a zero tolerance policy for excuses.

The Athlete's Responsibility

Regardless of the sport or activity, athletes have a broad range of responsibilities. Some include the following:

Tough Enough

- Training (i.e., skill development, conditioning, nutrition and supplementation, proper sleep, etc).
- Attitudes toward the game or sport.
- Attitudes towards teammates, coaches and spectators.
- Attitudes towards the opponent(s).
- Physical actions made during competition.
- Decisions made during competition.
- Arousal control during competition.
- Situational awareness during competition.
- Self-awareness before, during, and after competition.
- Evaluations or appraisals made after your performance.
- Conduct and behavior off the playing field (i.e., acting as a positive role model for others to emulate).

Courage

Courage is at the essential core of any hero. Courage both inspires and validates the warrior. In all times and in all places, courage has been admired and revered, and has become the reason and the rationale for a society's success. But precisely what is courage? In many ways, it is easier to say what courage is not. Courage is not recklessness or foolish risk-taking, nor is it haphazard rage and fury. Instead, courage breeds confidence, resolution, and bravery. As many a fighter will tell you, fear can be intimately entwined with courage. Fear is the stimulus that, biologically speaking, triggers the fight-or-flight response; yet courage is choosing to stay and fight rather than to run away.

Courage Requires Fear

Courage is not the absence of fear, rather it's the ability to perform difficult actions or tasks when you are frightened. It requires you to confront a host of negative emotions and sensations including fear, anxiety, pain, intimidation, and trepidation. As you can imagine, courage is an essential quality for both warriors and athletes.

However, acts of courage are not just limited to elite soldiers or world-class athletes. In fact, everyday living requires courage. Often courage is demonstrated by ordinary people from all walks of life. Take, for example, something as seemingly trivial as a small and insecure teenager confronting an intimidating bully at school or an awkward and unpopular boy asking a girl out on a date. Although small by comparison with major acts of heroism, these trivial actions can be extremely stressful because they require taking action in the face of fear, apprehension, and insecurity. Most importantly, these small acts of courage are critical because they serve as steppingstones to greater acts of courage in the future.

The Coward and the Hero

Both heroes and cowards alike experience fear. However, the difference between the two is how each one handles it. When a coward experiences fear he will either freeze in his tracks or try to escape from the threat or danger. Conversely, when a hero experiences fear, he confronts it head-on by taking positive actions to overcome the obstacle or challenge.

What is Fear?

Understanding fear and it's effects on your mind and body is the first step to managing it. Essentially, fear is a strong and unpleasant emotional reaction to a real or perceived threat. If uncontrolled, fear leads to panic. Then it's too late to adequately perform.

Three Levels of Fear

To prevent the negative effects of fear, you need to understand its levels and dynamics. For analysis, I have categorized fear into three different levels, listed in order of intensity:

- **Fright** – quick or sudden fear.
- **Panic** – overpowering fear.
- **Terror** – crippling or immobilizing fear.

While these three levels of fear vary in degrees of stress, they all have one common root response: the fight-or-flight response.

What is The Fight-or-Flight Response?

Whenever a person, or any animal for that matter, feels threatened or frightened, certain physiological changes occur. They start in the brain when the hypothalamus sends strong impulses to the pituitary gland, causing it to release a hormone (ACTH) that stimulates the adrenal glands to release other hormones into the bloodstream.

Ultimately every nerve and muscle is involved. This adrenaline will cause an increased heart rate with a corresponding increase in respiration and blood pressure. Your muscles will tense up, you will start to sweat, and your mouth will go dry. In addition, your digestive system will shut down to allow a better supply of blood to the muscles. Your hair will stand on end (piloerection). Your pupils will enlarge so that your vision can improve. Your hand and limbs will also begin to tremble. Once these biochemical mechanisms and processes are fully engaged – and it takes only nanoseconds – your body will be in the fight-or-flight mode.

Chapter 2: The Mental Toughness Package

Arousal Control

For most people, the fight-or-flight response has a debilitating effect. They panic or freeze up, and fear then becomes a powerful weapon of the opponent. Therefore, it is critically important that you learn to control the physiological and psychological response to make it work for you and not against you in a critical situation. This is referred to as "arousal control."

The first step to controlling arousal is to accept the fact that the fight-or-flight response is a natural human response. In fact, it's one of Mother Nature's best ways of helping you survive a stressful situation. You've got to take advantage of this assistance by using the energy of the adrenaline surge to augment your physical performance.

Second, harness the fight-or-flight response by preparing yourself thoroughly for the danger that may one day confront you. Developing the psychological and physical skills of your craft will lead to a personal self-confidence. In turn, this confidence leads to an inner calm. Inner calm is the environment necessary for peak performance.

Third, actively employ coping techniques like meditation, mental visualization, positive self-talk, and controlled breathing skills to manage the immediate effects of stress, anxiety, and fear.

Fourth, develop a keen sense of self-awareness. Never stop assessing your state of mind and reactions to different stressful situations. For example, the next time you are startled by something, pay close attention. What was it that startled you and why? Did you freeze up? What did you see? What did you hear? Were you trembling and breathing heavily? Was your mind clear or distracted? Exactly what were you thinking about? How much detail can you remember? Did you make any tactical errors in your responses? These are only a few of the questions you should answer over and over again as you go through the process of preparing yourself psychologically.

Another method of psychological preparation is written analysis. For example, write down five different hypothetical scenarios that truly frighten you. These scenarios could take place anywhere. Be specific with your details. Make certain to include the following relevant factors:

1. The source of danger and threat.
2. The time of day.
3. The environment.

Chapter 2: The Mental Toughness Package

4. Your mental, physical and emotional state during the crisis.
5. Any other relevant factors to your scenario.

Once you've completed these scenarios, have your coach or instructor identify the specific factors that elicit reasonable fear and then adjust your training to meet your concerns.

Possible Physiological Responses To Fear

- Enlarged pupils
- Dry mouth
- Trembling hands
- Cold, clammy hands
- Increased heart rate
- Shutdown of digestive system
- Tense muscles
- Sudden adrenaline surge
- Hair stands on end
- Enhanced alertness

How to Develop Courage

Courage is a tool that enables you to confront the fear. Like any tool, it can be developed and sharpened, so you'll be adequately prepared to deal with life's obstacles. When properly developed, courage gives you strength and empowerment to achieve your goal. It affords you the mental composure to perform risky and perhaps dangerous tasks with dignity and grace. Developing courage is a process that takes time. The goal is to take small steps that will progressively lead to significant acts of courage. What follows are a few guidelines to help you develop courage.

Tough Enough

1. First, understand that courage is not the absence of fear. It is action made in the face of fear.

2. Realize that courage is critical to your survival. Intellectualize the alternative – living a fearful life!

3. Make it a habit to listen to or read the daily news. Pay attention to all stories relating to acts of bravery and heroism.

4. If you ever have the opportunity, talk to military veterans, law enforcement officers, firefighters, and other types of emergency responders. Their real-life stories are truly inspiring and often filled with acts of courage.

5. Get into the habit of stepping out of your personal comfort zone. Do things that you wouldn't normally do. For example, if you are a shy person, make a daily goal to initiate a friendly conversation with a stranger. Or ask someone out on a date. Remember, the goal is to take baby steps that will progressively build up your courage.

6. If you are someone who plays role-playing video games, consider only playing "permanent death" or dead-is-dead versions of the game. While this might seem trivial to non-gamers, the consequences are huge for people who invest hundreds of hours of their lives playing a game. Playing dead-is-dead, compared to just reloading a saved game, brings an entirely new dimension to gaming. Every action has tremendous repercussions for the player. It's not unusual for many gamers who play dead-is-dead to experience intense emotions such as stress, anxiety, apprehension, and even trepidation.

7. Learn how to mask your fear. Masking is the process of "staying cool" and concealing your emotions from your opponent when you are experiencing fear or trepidation.

Chapter 2: The Mental Toughness Package

It is the process of manipulating and managing your body language (both facial expressions and body gestures). In many cases, displaying signs of fear, anger, trepidation or weariness will just fuel your opponent's fire. Unfortunately, masking cannot hide some involuntary physical reactions (i.e., excessive perspiring, heavy breathing, trembling hands, etc.). However, the good news is you can cover them up by quickly moving about, diverting the opponent's attention elsewhere, etc.

8. Regularly use coping techniques like meditation, mental visualization, positive self-talk, and controlled breathing skills to manage your fears.

9. Depending on your situation, you can use scenario-based training and other stress inoculation techniques to manage fear.

10. Strive to master the knowledge, skills and attitudes of your craft.

11. Understand and accept the physiological responses to the fight-or-flight response.

12. Evaluate your past responses to crisis situations. What did you do right? What did you do wrong?

Tough Enough

Chapter Three
Steps to Mental Toughness

Tough Enough

Chapter 3: Steps to Mental Toughness

Just Three Simple Steps

Mental toughness is both a mindset and skill that can be developed with proper training. However, before delving into the specifics, it's essential that you first begin by identifying and defining your training goals.

Step 1:

Now is the time to sit down and identify exactly what you want. What do you hope to accomplish by training for the next few months? Your goal can be anything. For example, do you want to lose weight in order to fight in a lower weight division? Build up your self-confidence? Beat a specific opponent? Beat your PR (personal record) in the gym? Become a heavy weight champion? Start now and write down all of the goals that you hope to achieve in the course of your training.

Step 2:

Once you have identified your goal, the next important step is to deconstruct and classify it into one of the following types of goal categories.

- **Micro goal** – A micro goal is a long-term goal deconstructed into smaller task-specific objectives.
- **Short-term goal** – Represents something you want to accomplish in a few hours or a day.
- **Mid-term goal** – Represents something you want to achieve in a few days or a few weeks.
- **Long-term goal** – Represents something you ultimately want to achieve in the future. Long-term goals often take months and even years to achieve.

Step 3:

Once you have identified a very specific goal and have broken it down into micro-goals, the next step is to commit yourself to it. Remember, goals are useless unless you put them into action.

Every day, you've got to set aside some time from your busy schedule to actively pursue these micro-goals. There simply is no way around it. The good news is, the more you hold yourself to these small goals, the closer you'll get to realize your long term objective. Moreover, you'll improve both your self-discipline and self-confidence at the same time.

One of the best ways to stay on track is to remind yourself constantly of your goals. Get into the habit of posting your daily micro-goals in places where you are likely to see them. For example, post reminder notes in places like the bathroom mirror, on your refrigerator door, on your bedroom nightstand, and the edge of your computer's monitor. If you're more of a gadget type of person, there are dozens of reminder and to-do apps available for your computer, tablet, and smartphone. These simple yet effective reminders will keep you organized, motivated, and focused on your goals throughout the day.

Mental Toughness Training

To reap the full benefits of mental toughness training, you have to reproduce both physiological and psychological stressors. Once again, your objective is to cope, perform and prevail from each stressful training event.

In addition, mental toughness exercises must be demanding and possibly lead to performance degradation. They must challenge and activate the individual building blocks of mental toughness.

Stress inoculation training is invaluable for developing the mental

Chapter 3: Steps to Mental Toughness

strength necessary to handle various types of stress. As a result, you'll experience less anxiety and fewer performance failures.

Finally, mental toughness training is not a substitute for skill development required by your particular sport, occupation, or discipline. It is supplemental to a foundational skill development program. However, if you have concerns about integrating mental toughness training with your current training program, consider talking with your trainer, coach, or instructor.

To reap the full benefits of mental toughness training, you have to reproduce both physiological and psychological stressors.

Physiological or Psychological Stressors

Stress and adversity come in many different forms. However, there are two broad categories of stressors: physiological or psychological. A physiological stressor is something that puts strain

Tough Enough

on your body. It can be an injury, the sensation of pain, fatigue, or illness. A physiological stressor can also come from environmental factors such as sudden loud noises, poor lighting conditions, uneven or unstable terrain, extreme temperatures, etc.

In contrast, a psychological stressor is anything your brain interprets as harmful or threatening, and it can be caused by situations, events, circumstances, or individuals. Moreover, a psychological stressor can tax the cognitive and emotional systems of the brain.

Mental toughness exercises can also be used to test the strength and resilience of individuals. Pictured here, BUD/S (Basic Underwater Demolition/SEAL) Training at Naval Amphibious Base Coronado.

Therefore, a beneficial mental toughness exercise should produce anyone of six types of stressors during the training event. They include:

- **Acute emotional stress**
- **Mental confusion**

Chapter 3: Steps to Mental Toughness

- Mental fatigue
- Physical fatigue (muscular or aerobic)
- Physical discomfort or pain
- Environmental stress

Now that you understand the requirements for a mental toughness exercise, let's look at the different drills you'll be using in your program.

Mental Toughness Exercises

In the next two chapters, I'm going to teach you a variety of mental toughness exercises that will help you achieve peak performance in all of your endeavors. They include both physical and cognitive drills that will expose you to many different types of stressors. Many of these exercises can be performed individually, while others will require the assistance of a training partner, instructor or coach.

A word of caution! Before you begin any exercise program, including the ones featured in this book, make certain that you have been cleared by your doctor.

Tough Enough

Chapter Four
Physical Training for Mental Toughness

Tough Enough

Chapter 4: Physical Training Mental Toughness

The Importance of Contact Drills

The mental toughness exercises featured in this chapter were developed over the course of thirty plus years of teaching the fighting arts. You will discover that most of the drills and exercises are "combat-oriented." This is intentional for three principal reasons.

First, in order to adequately develop the mental toughness attributes, your training must be extremely intense and realistic. Compared to other forms of training, combat drills are the most demanding because they instantly create both physiological and psychological stressors. For instance, combat simulation exercises often present all six elements of extreme adversity, including danger, risk, fear, loss, pain, and self-confidence. In order for you to complete a combat-oriented drill, you must give it everything you've got!

In this photo, two soldiers engage in pugil stick fighting.

Second, warriors who perform high-risk duties will find these drills invaluable for their occupations. Soldiers, law enforcement officers, security agents, and self-defense practitioners will acquire specific mental toughness attributes, while simultaneously developing

59

Tough Enough

life-saving fighting skills.

However, reality is the key ingredient, and you must always practice and train the way you want to react in a high-stress situation. In fact, I often tell my students, "train the way you want to fight and fight the way you train." In other words, you must methodically and safely integrate the frightening and spontaneous elements of fighting into your training program. Remember, under stress, you will instinctively revert to the way you have been trained.

For example, in my classes, I have students participate in dozens of scenario-based drills using a variety of equipment and environmental props. Since no two attacks are ever the same, I am constantly changing the combat scenarios in my program. When all is said and done, this realistic and dynamic form of stress inoculation training provides my students with the experience and confidence necessary to handle the volatile and unpredictable nature of combat.

Third, athletes from all sports will benefit from combat-oriented drills. Regardless of your sport or level of play, these exercises will make you a much better athlete. It has been said that martial arts training is the foundation for all sports, and rightly so. The martial arts tap into every single physical attribute necessary for peak sports performance. Some attributes including: speed, quickness, power, coordination, agility, timing, aerobic conditioning, distancing, ambidexterity, endurance, flexibility, tactile sensitivity, kinesthetic perception, pain tolerance, awareness, finesse, accuracy, and non-telegraphic movement.

As a matter of fact, the NFL recognizes the importance of martial arts cross-training. For example, NFL teams such as the Dallas Cowboys, Kansas City Chiefs, Miami Dolphins, Green Bay Packers, and Denver Broncos have used martial arts training for skill development.

Chapter 4: Physical Training Mental Toughness

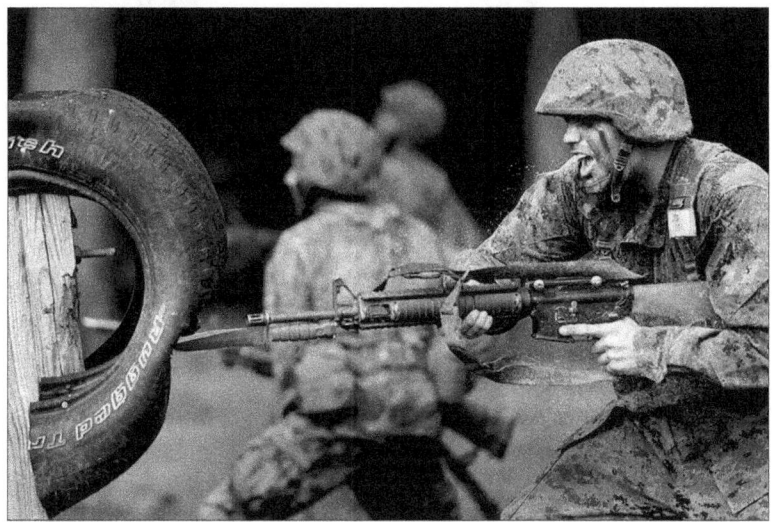

While the bayonet is seldom used on today's battlefield, it's an important tool for developing instrumental aggression in soldiers. In this photo, a Marine recruit goes through the bayonet assault training course at Parris Island, South Carolina.

Got Fighting Skills?

You don't have to be a Navy SEAL, martial artist or self-defense expert to perform many of the exercises featured in this book. However, there are some basic fighting skills you'll need to know if you want to get the most out of your training. Some skills include the fighting stance, kicking and punching techniques, and various defensive maneuvers.

For this purpose, I have included step-by-step instructions for performing these necessary skills. You can find them in the appendix of this book. Nevertheless, if you still need help with these foundational techniques, consider taking an introductory boxing, mixed martial arts or self-defense class.

61

Tough Enough

Pictured here, two U.S. Marines practice ground fighting techniques in a martial arts program on Forward Operating Base Shir Ghazay, Helmand province,

Warming Up

Before beginning any of the drills, it's important that you first warm up and stretch out. Warming up slowly increases the internal temperature of your body while stretching improves your workout performance, keeps you flexible, and helps reduce the possibility of an injury.

Some of the best exercises for warming up are jumping jacks, rope skipping or a short jog before training. Another effective method of warming up your muscles is to perform light and easy movements with the weights.

When stretching out, keep in mind that all movements should be performed in a slow and controlled manner. Try to hold your stretch for a minimum of sixty seconds and avoid all bouncing movements. You should feel mild tension on the muscle that is being stretched.

Chapter 4: Physical Training Mental Toughness

Remember to stay relaxed and focus on what you are doing. Here are seven stretches:

- **Neck stretch** – from a comfortable standing position, slowly tilt your head to the right side of your neck, holding it for a count of twenty. Then tilt your head to the left side for approximately twenty seconds. Stretch each side of the neck at least three times.

- **Triceps stretch** – from a standing position, keep your knees slightly bent, extend your right arm overhead, hold the elbow of your right arm with your left hand, and slowly pull your right elbow to the left. Keep your hips straight as you stretch your triceps gently for thirty seconds. Repeat this stretch for the other arm.

- **Hamstring stretch** – from a seated position on the floor, extend your right leg in front of you with your toe pointing to the ceiling. Place the sole of your left foot in the inside of your extended leg. Gently lean forward at the hips and stretch out the hamstrings of your right leg. Hold this position for a minimum of sixty seconds. Switch legs and repeat the stretch.

- **Spinal twist** – from a seated position on the floor, extend your right leg in front of you. Raise your left leg and place it on the outside of your right leg. Place your right elbow on the outside of your left thigh. Stabilize your stretch with your elbow and twist your upper body and head to your left side. Breathe naturally and hold this stretch for a minimum of thirty seconds. Switch legs and repeat this stretch for the other side.

- **Quad stretch** – assume a sitting position on the floor with your hamstrings folded and resting on top of your calves. Your toes should be pointed behind you, and your instep should be flush with the ground. Sit comfortably into the stretch and hold for a minimum of sixty seconds.
- **Prone stretch** – lay on the ground with your back to the floor. Exhale as you straighten your arms and legs. Your fingers and toes should be stretching in opposite directions. Hold this stretch for thirty seconds.
- **Groin stretch** – sit on the ground with the soles of your feet touching each other. Grab hold of your feet and slowly pull yourself forward until mild tension is felt in your groin region. Hold this position for a minimum of sixty seconds.

Physical Exercises for Mental Toughness

In this chapter, I'm going to teach you specific drills and exercises for developing mental toughness that will yield fantastic results in boxing and mixed martial arts. Most of them are the culmination of years of research, analysis, and experimentation. I have used these exercises to teach thousands of students over the past three decades and I'm confident they will help you in your training.

Impact Training

Impact training is a series of physical exercises designed to condition your mind and body to withstand the trauma of strikes and blows. It's also effective for developing mental resilience, attention

Chapter 4: Physical Training Mental Toughness

control, and self-confidence.

In unarmed combat, there are two types of striking impact: snapping and breaking. Snapping impact shocks the head or body but does not fully penetrate it. It's quick but lacks substantial follow-through. A snapping blow usually makes a brisk, sharp cracking sound when it connects with its target. In contrast, breaking impact shocks and moves the head or body. It can break or fracture bones easily because it follows through its target (approximately three inches). You must be physically and psychologically prepared to tolerate both types of impact.

Impact training requires both forms of impact to be administered to specific body parts, including the shoulders, back, chest, biceps, triceps, abdominals, thighs, and calves. Striking these targets will not cause severe or permanent injury. *Never strike the face, neck, throat, solar plexus, spine, groin, or joints during impact training.* These anatomical targets are very sensitive and cannot be conditioned to withstand deliberate impact. Striking these targets can cause severe and permanent injury. It is imperative that your training partner deliver accurate blows and avoid these targets during training.

For impact training, your training partner will need a pair of boxing gloves or focus mitts to deliver the blows. When you begin, have your partner start off slowly with light strikes to your muscle groups, alternating snapping and breaking blows. Always remember to exhale when the blow makes contact. Over time, your partner can increase the speed and force of the strikes. Be patient with each other. It will take time and some experimentation before you and your partner can correctly gauge the amount of power. Impact training sessions should last approximately five minutes and should be conducted at least twice a month.

Medicine Ball Drill

Medicine Ball training develops mental resilience, self-confidence, and attention control. When used properly, it also promotes proper breathing, physical endurance, and the ability to withstand powerful blows to the body.

One of the best ways to train with the medicine ball is to have a training partner repeatedly throw it into your stomach while you are either standing or lying down on your back. Remember to exhale and flex your abdominal muscles when the ball is forcefully thrown into your body.

A good workout would include a two minute round with one-minute rest period. Depending on your level of conditioning and specific training goals, you might do this for a total of 4 rounds. A word of caution, however, medicine ball training is hard on the body, so practice no more than two times per week.

Chapter 4: Physical Training Mental Toughness

Full-Contact Sparring

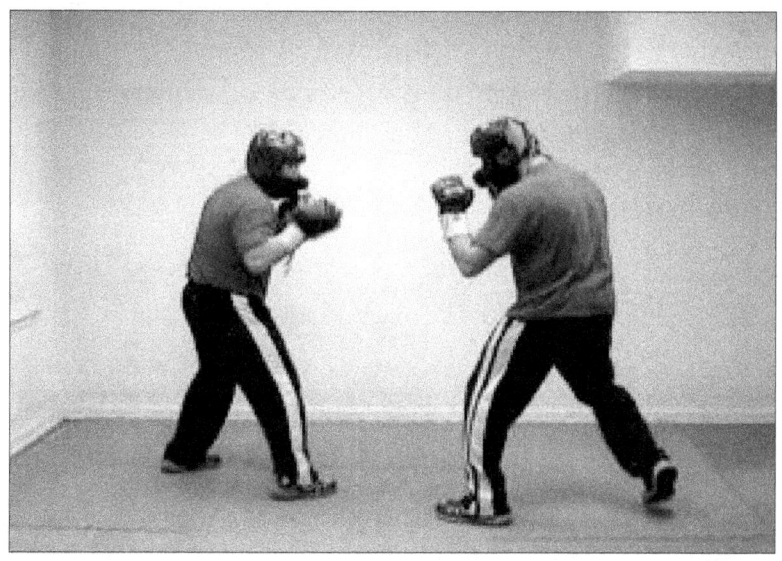

Full-contact sparring is a practical method for developing instrumental aggression, attention control, self-confidence, immediate resilience, and arousal control. It also develops many physical attributes like speed, quickness, coordination, agility, timing, distancing, ambidexterity, endurance, flexibility, tactile sensitivity, pain tolerance, finesse, accuracy, and non-telegraphic movement.

Sparring skills require combining punches into fluid and logical combinations. Basic sparring sessions are conducted at a moderate and controlled pace. The good news is you can spar just about anywhere, such as a gym, basement, garage and even outdoors. However, before you begin training, you'll need protective head gear, 14 oz boxing gloves, and a mouth piece.

Depending on your level of conditioning, sparring rounds can range anywhere from one to five minutes. Each round is separated by either 30-second, one-minute or two-minute breaks. A good sparring session consists of at least five to eight rounds.

67

Tough Enough

Since sparring workouts are structured around time, you will need a good workout timer. Most workout timers will allow you to adjust your round lengths anywhere from 30 seconds to 9 minutes. Rest periods can be changed from 30 seconds to 5 minutes depending on your level of conditioning and training goals.

When You Get Hit!

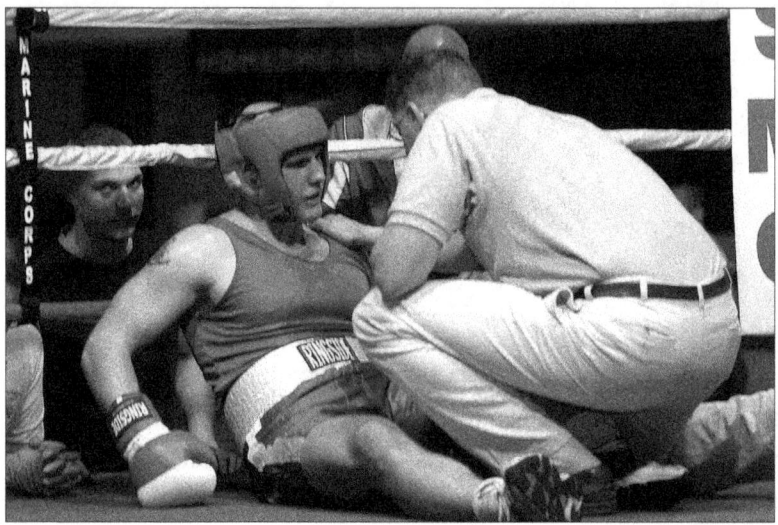

If and when you get hit in a sparring session, stay in control of your emotions and don't panic. Keep both hands up, stay mobile, and remain defensively alert. Maintain proper breathing, employ positive self-talk, and don't allow negative thoughts to contaminate your mind. Stay focused on the task at hand and continue to look for openings in your training partner's defenses.

Here are ten common mistakes that are made when sparring. Overcoming these errors will significantly enhance your mental toughness attributes.

1. Quitting or giving up after being hit.
2. Being distracted (internally or externally) when fighting.

Chapter 4: Physical Training Mental Toughness

3. Fearful or excessive blinking.
4. Randomly throwing punches or failing to focus on a particular target.
5. Lack of commitment when attacking your partner.
6. Hesitating or over thinking.
7. Turning your head away or closing your eyes when a blow is thrown at you.
8. Turning your body completely sideways from the sparring partner.
9. Running away from your opponent's attack.
10. Nervously swatting your sparring partner's boxing glove.

Handicapped Sparring

Handicapped sparring develops immediate resilience, attention control, self-confidence and arousal control while sharpening and refining individual fighting techniques. This form of restricted sparring is conducted by having one person spar with only one arm at a time. For example, during the course of a three-minute round, you are restricted to attacking and defending with only your right arm while your training partner can spar with both of his limbs.

Handicapped sparring can also include fighting opponents who are significantly larger than you. For example, see what it is like to spar someone who is two feet taller than you, or experience what it's like to exchange punches with someone who is 100 pounds heavier than you. These different types opponents will create the necessary mental and physical stressors to improve your mental toughness.

Hip Fusing Drill

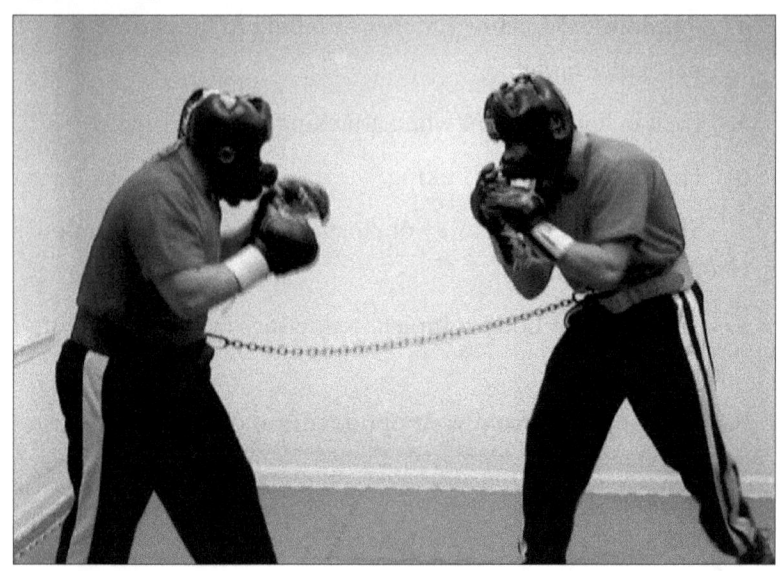

Hip fusing is an advanced form of sparring that develops attention control, instrumental aggression, self-confidence, immediate resilience, and arousal control.

Hip fusing requires tethering yourself to your partner with a heavy-duty chain. To perform the hip fusing drill, place a weight lifting belt on each participant. Next, attach a heavy-duty chain (approximately 4 feet in length) to each belt. The length of the chain will depend on your skill level. For example, a longer chain would be used for beginners who need more defensive reaction time to defend against the blows.

A word of caution: Prematurely engaging in hip fusing drills can be dangerous and counterproductive. Remember, hip fusing is for advanced practitioners who have a solid foundation in full-contact sparring. Never participate in hip fusing until you have acquired the following skills:

Chapter 4: Physical Training Mental Toughness

1. A strong foundation in offense and defensive skills.
2. The ability to control the force of your offensive techniques.
3. The fundamental attributes of unarmed combat (i.e. speed, timing, coordination, accuracy, balance, and the ability not to telegraph your movements
4. A safe attitude toward training.

Circle Combat

Circle combat develops several mental toughness attributes, including self-confidence, immediate resilience, situational awareness, selective attention, and arousal control.

This drill is conducted by having approximately 5 participants form a large circle (approximately 12 feet in diameter) around one person standing in the center. All of the participants must wear protective gear.

The drill begins with the instructor randomly selecting participants from the circle to attack the person in the middle. The defender must immediately identify and react to the attack using various defensive skills and techniques. Once the attacker finishes his assault, he returns to the circle, and the instructor immediately calls out another attacker. Once the practitioners become familiar with this drill, the instructor can make it more difficult by speeding up the selection of attackers, calling out multiple attackers at once, and even having the attackers take the fight to the ground (for Mixed Martial Arts only) . Circle combat can last anywhere from 30 seconds to 5 minutes. It's up to the coach and the student's level of conditioning.

The Three Training Methodologies

There are three specific training methodologies used to develop mental toughness, as well as the fundamental skills of armed and unarmed fighting. They are proficiency training, conditioning training, and street training.

Proficiency Training

Proficiency training develops important attributes like self-discipline, immediate resilience, and attention control. When conducted properly, it also develops speed, power, accuracy, non-telegraphic movement, balance, and psychomotor skills. The training objective is to sharpen one specific body weapon, maneuver, or technique at a time by executing it over and over for a prescribed number of repetitions. Each time the technique is executed with clean form at various speeds. Movements can also be performed with your eyes closed to develop a kinesthetic feel for the action.

Proficiency training can be accomplished through the use of various types of equipment, including the heavy bag, double-end bag, focus mitts, striking shields and so on.

Conditioning Training

The next methodology is conditioning training, and it's used for developing self-confidence and immediate resilience. Conditioning training also develops endurance, fluidity, rhythm, distancing, timing, speed, footwork, and balance.

Conditioning training can be performed on various pieces

Chapter 4: Physical Training Mental Toughness

of equipment, including the heavy bag, double-end bag, focus mitts, body opponent bag, and against imaginary assailants in shadowboxing.

In most cases, conditioning training requires the practitioner to deliver a variety of fighting combinations for three or four-minute rounds separated by 30-second breaks. Like proficiency training, this type of training can also be performed at various speeds. A good workout consists of at least five rounds. Conditioning training is not necessarily limited to just three or four-minute rounds. For example, in some of my classes, I will have advanced students ground fighting for 30 minutes or longer.

Street Training (for self-defense training only)

Street training is primarily used for developing instrumental aggression. However, it also improves speed, power, explosiveness, target selection and recognition, timing, footwork, pacing, and breath control.

Street training prepares you for the sudden stress and immediate fatigue of a real fight. Since many violent altercations are explosive, lasting an average of twenty seconds, you must train for this possible scenario. This means delivering explosive and powerful compound attacks with vicious intent for approximately twenty seconds, resting one minute, and then repeating the process.

You should practice this training methodology in different lighting, on different terrains, and in different environmental settings. You can use different types of training equipment as well. For example, you can prepare yourself for multiple assailants by having your training partners attack you with focus mitts from a variety of angles, ranges, and target postures. For twenty seconds, go after them with vicious low-line kicks, powerful punches, and devastating strikes.

Focus Mitt Training

Focus mitt training develops several mental toughness attributes, including instrumental aggression, resilience, self-confidence, awareness, and attention control. It also improves defensive skills, accuracy, speed, target recognition, target selection, target impact, and timing in all offensive techniques.

The focus mitt (also called punching mitt or focus pad) is an exceptional piece of training equipment that can be used by anyone. By placing the mitts at various angles and levels, you can perform every conceivable kick, punch, or strike known to mankind. Properly utilized, focus mitts will refine your defensive reaction time and condition your entire body for combat.

Focus mitts are constructed of durable leather designed to withstand tremendous punishment. Compared to other pieces of equipment, the focus mitt is relatively inexpensive. However, an effective workout requires two mitts (one for each hand). Your training partner (called the feeder) plays a vital role in focus mitt workouts by controlling the techniques you execute and the cadence of delivery. The intensity of your workouts will depend largely upon

Chapter 4: Physical Training Mental Toughness

his or her ability to manipulate the mitts and push you to your limit. I often tell my students that a good focus mitt feeder is one step ahead of his training partner, whereas a great focus mitt feeder is two steps ahead of his partner.

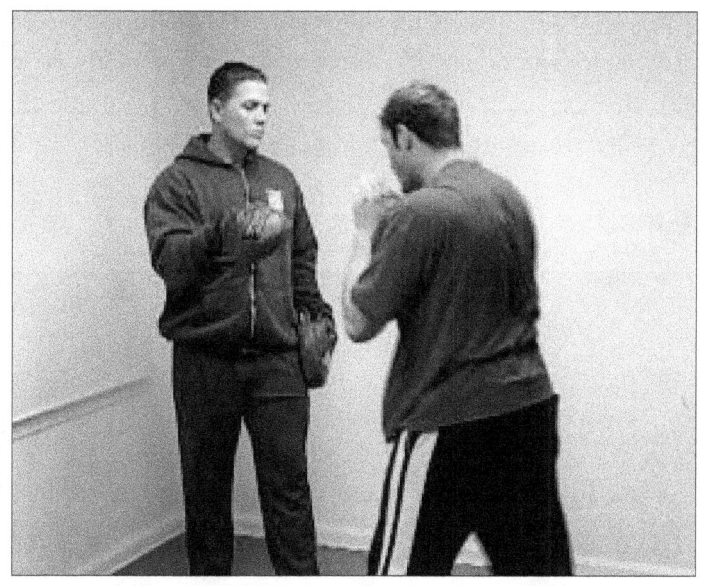

When training with your partner, give them constructive feedback and let them know how he or she is doing. Remember, communication is vital during your workout sessions. Also, try to avoid remaining stationary. Get into the habit of constantly moving around with quick, economical steps.

To truly benefit from any focus mitt workout, you must learn to concentrate intensely throughout the entire session. You must block out both internal and external distractions. Try to visualize the focus mitt as a living, breathing assailant, not an inanimate target. This type of visualization will make the difference between a poor workout and a great training session. You also might want to draw small Xs on the mitts. This practice will improve your focus and concentration and help you develop accurate striking techniques.

Tough Enough

All three training methodologies (proficiency training, conditioning training, and street training) can also be applied to the focus mitts. For example, if you applied the street training methodology you can prepare yourself for a ballistic street assault by having your training partner attack you with focus mitts from a variety of angles and ranges of combat. For twenty seconds, go after him with vicious and devastating strikes. Rest for one minute and then go again. The training possibilities are truly endless.

The Gauntlet Drill

The gauntlet drill builds instrumental aggression, mental resilience, attention control and situational awareness. To perform this exercise, you will need a minimum of ten people, each one holding a focus mitt. Divide the ten people into two equal rows and make certain they hold the glove at approximately head level.

Next, have the designated striker start from the top of the rows. From a fighting stance, have him deliver a lead straight/rear cross combination in a crisscross fashion while steadily moving down the

Chapter 4: Physical Training Mental Toughness

two rows. Once he works his way through the "gauntlet," he should quickly return to the starting position (top of the row) and begins again. A good workout would be to perform this drill for 10 minutes non-stop.

Heavy Bag Training

Heavy bag training builds instrumental aggression, immediate resilience, self-confidence, and attention control. Heavy bag work is regularly used in boxing, kick boxing, mixed martial arts, and self-defense. It is also popular among people who just want to stay in shape or add a new dimension to their fitness programs. Many people use the heavy bag for some of the following reasons:

- It conditions the entire body.
- It improves muscular endurance.
- It strengthens bones, tendons, and ligaments.
- It conditions the cardiovascular system.
- It relieves stress and helps channel aggressive energy.

77

Tough Enough

The heavy bag is constructed of either top grain leather, canvas or vinyl. Most bags are 14 inches in diameter and 42 inches in length. The interior of the bag is filled with either cotton fiber, thick foam, sand or other durable material. Depending on the brand, heavy bags can weigh anywhere from seventy-five to two hundred and fifty pounds. However, for our purposes, I suggest a bag that weighs a minimum of 150 pounds.

Safe and effective heavy bag training will require you to find a place that will allow both you and the bag to move around freely. The location should also be a relatively quiet place that is free of distractions. Here are a few places you might want to consider:

- Garage
- Carport
- Basement
- Barn
- Home gym (if you are fortunate enough)
- Open field or backyard
- Warehouse
- Under a deck

Before you begin working out, invest in a good pair of bag gloves that will protect your hands when working out. When buying gloves, spare no expense and look for a reputable and high-quality brand. This will provide years of reliable use and will help ensure a better quality workout.

If you don't think you'll need bag gloves, think again. Striking the heavy bag without hand protection causes sore knuckles, bruised bones, hand inflammation, sore wrists and scraped knuckles. As a result, it will set your training back for several weeks in order for your hands to heal.

Chapter 4: Physical Training Mental Toughness

A good heavy bag workout consists of at least five rounds lasting three minutes in duration. However, you can also apply the other two methodologies (proficiency and street training) to your routine. Here are some important tips when working out on the bag:

1. Always warm up with some light stretching and calisthenics before working out.
2. Gradually build up the force of your blows. Remember, a beginner's wrists are too weak to accommodate full-force punches.
3. Never sacrifice balance for power.
4. Remember to snap your punches.
5. Always keep your wrists straight when striking the bag.
6. Always maintain proper form.
7. Move around and avoid remaining stationary.
8. Learn to integrate your kicks, punches, and strikes into logical compound attacks.
9. Pace yourself to avoid premature exhaustion.
10. Don't wear jewelry or a watch when training.
11. Stay relaxed and avoid unnecessary muscular tension.
12. Never hold your breath. Remember to exhale with the delivery of each and every technique.
13. Avoid the urge to stop the bag from moving. Let it swing freely!
14. If you don't know the proper way to throw a punch or kick, get instruction from a qualified coach or instructor.
15. Avoid heavy bag training two days in a row. Give your body a few days to recover from your last workout.

The Pummel Drill (for MMA only)

The pummel drill develops instrumental aggression, immediate resilience, and self-confidence. Pummeling requires you to attack a heavy bag or body opponent bag with a flurry of strikes from the top mounted position for specified period of time. To execute the pummel drill, apply the following steps:

1. Place a heavy bag on the floor.

2. Have your training partner tie a rope (approximately five feet long) to the top of the bag.

3. Mount the heavy bag (the same way you would mount an assailant in a ground fight).

4. For 30 seconds employ full-speed, full-force strikes on the upper portion of the heavy bag. Be vicious and attack the back with all of the aggression you can muster. There are two punches that can be delivered effectively from this position: linear punches and hammer fist strikes.

Chapter 4: Physical Training Mental Toughness

5. Have your training partner pull vigorously (side to side, and up and down) on the rope while you deliver the blows. Strive to maintain a good base and avoid losing your balance when your partner tugs the bag.
6. Rest for one minute, and then repeat the process for a total of 10 sets.

The Elevation Drill

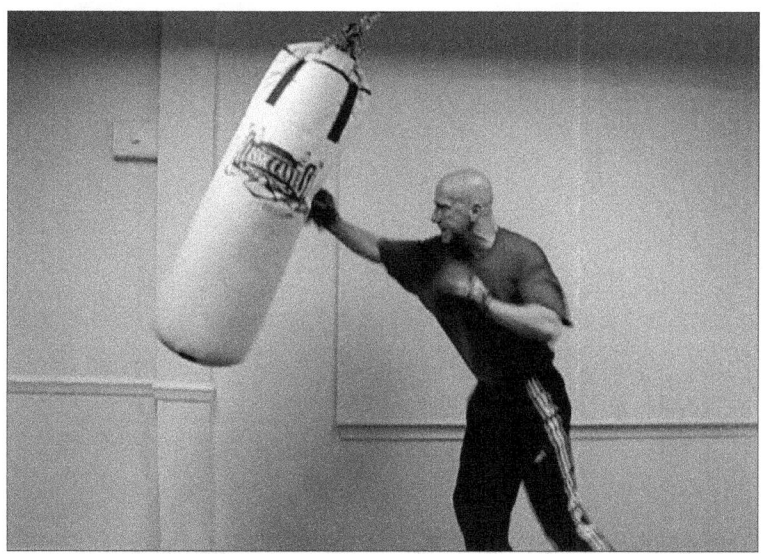

The elevation drill develops power punching skills while building instrumental aggression, mental resilience, and attention control. The objective of this exercise is to keep the heavy bag elevated at a 45-degree angle by continuously punching it. This drill is brutal on the arms. In fact, the average person can barely last 30 seconds. To perform the exercise follow these steps:

1. Face the heavy bag and assume a fighting stance.
2. Deliver the lead straight and rear cross combination continuously. Concentrate on delivering full-speed, full-force

punches.

3. Maintain a rapid-fire cadence to keep the bag elevated at a 45-degree angle from the floor.
4. Avoid pushing the bag, remember to snap each blow.
5. Perform the drill for a total of 5 rounds. Each round should last anywhere from 30 to 60 seconds. If you are exceptionally conditioned, go for 90 seconds.

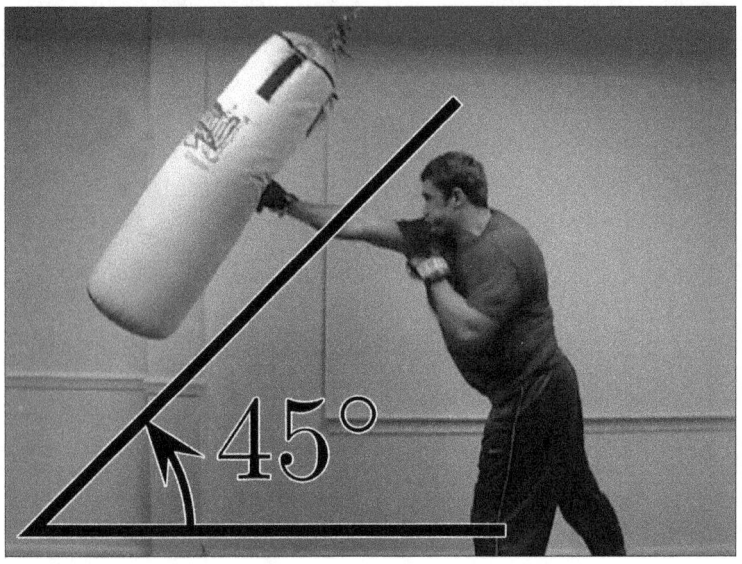

When performing the elevation drill, strive to maintain a rapid-fire cadence so the bag is elevated at a 45-degree angle from the floor.

Chapter 4: Physical Training Mental Toughness

The Head-Hunter Drill

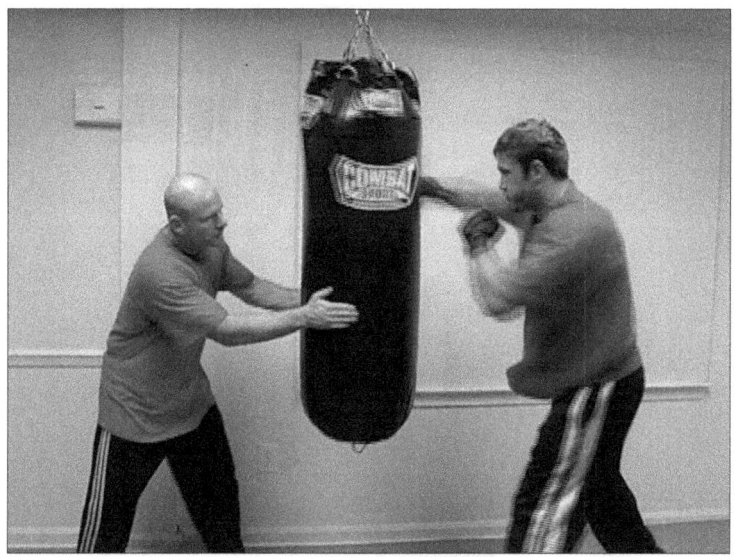

The head-hunter drill is a spin-off from the street training methodology. It is designed to sharpen and develop hook punches while building instrumental aggression, mental resilience, attention control and situational awareness.

1. To perform the drill, assume a fighting stance and square off in front of a heavy bag or focus mitts.
2. Next, execute a lead and rear hook combination (back and forth) with maximum power and speed for 30 seconds.
3. Don't stop attacking your target until the time has elapsed.
4. Rest for approximately 1 minute and then go again for five to ten rounds.
5. Be forewarned! This drill is exhausting.

Tough Enough

Shadowboxing

Shadowboxing is the creative deployment of offensive and defensive techniques against imaginary assailants. It requires intense mental concentration, honest self-analysis, and a deep commitment to improving you fighting skills. Regular shadowboxing develops instrumental aggression, resilience, self-confidence, and attention control.

For someone on a tight budget, the good news is that shadowboxing is inexpensive. All you need is a full-length mirror and a place to work out. The mirror is vital. It functions as a critic, your personal instructor. If you're honest, the mirror will be too. It will point out every mistake – telegraphing, sloppy footwork, poor body

Chapter 4: Physical Training Mental Toughness

mechanics, and even lack of physical conditioning.

Proper shadowboxing also develops speed, power, balance, footwork, compound attack skills, sound form, and finesse. It even promotes a better understanding of the ranges of combat. As you progress, you can incorporate light dumbbells or a weight vest into shadowboxing workouts to enhance power and speed.

A good shadowboxing workout consists of at least five rounds lasting three minutes in duration. Don't forget that you can also apply the proficiency and street training methodologies to your routine.

360-Degree Blocking Drill

The 360-degree blocking drill develops resilience, situational awareness, and attention control. To perform the exercise, apply the following steps:

Have your training partner stand approximately three feet from you.

Position yourself in a 45-degree fighting stance with both of your arms relaxed and hanging at your sides.

Without your partner telegraphing his intentions, have him deliver a random swing at your head or torso.

Immediately respond with the appropriate block.

Return your arm back to the starting position.

Have your partner immediately attack with another swing at a different angle.

As you become more proficient with this defensive drill, your training partner should deliver a sequence of random swings with greater speed and force. In addition, you can have your partner incorporate linear blows into the drill. Just remember to start out slowly and progressively build up the speed and force of your strikes.

Sidestepping Drill

The sidestepping drill improves both situational awareness and attention control. It also develops your sense of distance and timing. To practice the sidestepping exercise, employ the following:

1. Begin with your training partner standing approximately 10 feet from you.
2. Assume a fighting stance.
3. Without telegraphing his movement, your training partner should charge at you full speed.
4. If you're standing in a right stance, quickly step with your right foot to the right and have your left leg follow an equal distance.
5. When performed correctly, your partner should miss your body, and you should be in a balanced and ready position.
6. If your training partner runs into you, it's because you are moving too slowly. To remedy this problem, keep your weight evenly distributed and explode off the balls of your feet.
7. If your training partner tracks you, it's because you are moving too soon. To remedy this problem, avoid premature movements and wait until the very last second before you explode laterally.
8. Finally, you can practice the sidestepping drill with different stances, at various distances, in different lighting conditions, and while wearing a weight vest.

Chapter 4: Physical Training Mental Toughness

Disability Training

Disability training develops immediate resilience, situational awareness, and attention control. The goal is to experience what it's like to fight when you are under the weather or temporarily handicapped. Here are a few suggestions that will help get you started.

- Practice shadowboxing when you're plagued with a migraine headache.
- Practice close-quarter fighting techniques when confined to a wheelchair (for self-defense training only).
- Spar with one arm in a sling.
- Practice blocking and parrying skills while standing on crutches.
- Perform proficiency training on the heavy bag when you have the flu.
- Perform endurance push ups when you have a bad cough.
- Ground fighting when you are feeling fatigued or exhausted.
- Perform the circle combat drill when you are suffering from a hangover.
- Practice escaping from grabs, chokes, locks, and holds while you are blindfolded.
- Spar while wearing a weight vest.
- Wear an elevation training mask when working out on the heavy bag.
- Want to experience some real physical discomfort, try sparring with a marble in your shoe.

Adverse Weather & Unstable Terrain Training

Training outdoors in adverse weather conditions and working out on different types of unstable terrain will also build mental toughness. Here are a few suggestions:

- Perform endurance push-ups in the rain.
- Work out on the focus mitts without gloves during the freezing winter temperatures.
- Execute compound attacks in hot, humid summer weather.
- Conduct shadowboxing in the snow or mud.
- Spar when it's foggy outside.
- Practice kicking techniques in gusty winds.
- Grapple and ground fight in the dark.
- Practice knife defense skills in poor lighting conditions.
- Try speed-loading your gun when your hands are wet from rain.
- Perform gun disarming skills with the sun in your eyes.

Unstable Terrain

- Try sparring in tall grass.
- Try focus mitt training on the ice (be careful).
- Perform kicking techniques on wet pavement or grass. (MMA)
- Ground fight in the heavy wet snow. (MMA)
- Practice the sidestepping drill on gravel or mud.
- Practice hip fusing in the sand.

Chapter 4: Physical Training Mental Toughness

Weight Vest Training

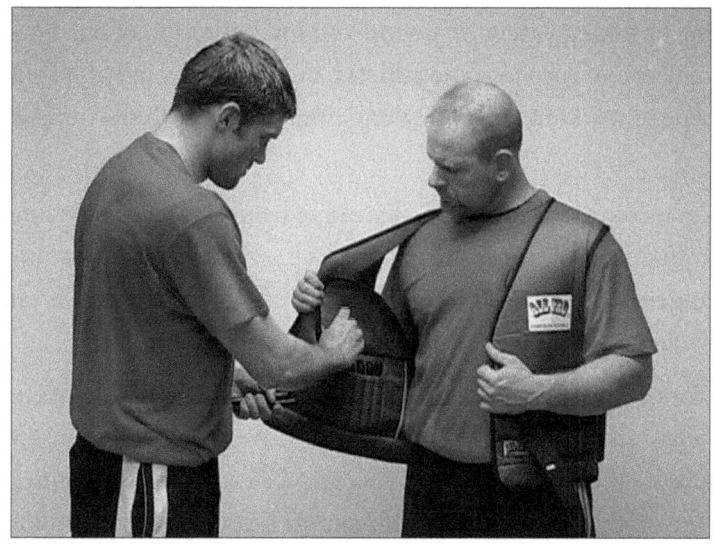

Weight vest training is unmatched for developing mental resilience. However, in order to get the best results from your workout, you'll need to invest in a high-quality vest that provides both comfort and durability. The vest must also be able to support a significant amount of weight, ranging anywhere from 50-150 pounds.

While there are countless high-intensity-short-duration workouts that can be performed with a weight vest, mental toughness training requires moderate intensity long duration workouts. Weight vest training for mental toughness resiliency has only three requirements:

1. You must carry enough weight to create immediate and significant stress on your body.
2. The physical stress and strain must be continuous and uninterrupted.
3. The workout session should be performed for a prolonged period, ranging anywhere from 45 to 60 minutes in duration.

Tough Enough

One of the best ways to achieve these requirements is by taking extended walks in various types of environments. For example, try walking or hiking with a 75-pound vest for a duration of one hour. This may sound easy to some athletes, but I assure you that it is not. This type of workout is grueling and draining on both the mind and body.

If possible, train outdoors, instead of using a treadmill. While the treadmill does have some advantages, (i.e., when weather conditions are dangerous, or when training outside isn't an option, etc.) it can also be detrimental to your mental toughness training.

Working out on a treadmill always gives you the option of ending your workout prematurely. For example, if you get tired because you bit off more than you can chew, you can always hit the stop button and take off the vest. Knowing this simple fact creates a psychological comfort zone that makes the activity less daunting.

On the other hand, outdoor training is more unsettling. You are exposed to the elements, extreme temperatures, and unpredictable terrain. Most importantly, outdoor training doesn't provide you with the luxury of quitting prematurely. You don't have the option of stopping and taking off your vest. In essence, you must finish what you started.

A word of caution. Weight vest training is extremely demanding on the body. Be very careful when starting out. Always begin with a small amount of weight and progressively add more over time. Never train with a lot of weight. Remember, your body needs time to adapt to the weight. Finally, be certain to speak to your doctor first to see if you have any condition that might be aggravated by this type of training.

Chapter 4: Physical Training Mental Toughness

Physical Fitness & Nutrition

There is no escaping the fact that the human mind and body are intrinsically linked to one another. Mental toughness requires that your mind and body work harmoniously together as a single well-oiled machine. All of its components must work efficiently and synchronize properly if you want to achieve optimal performance in any endeavor. Real mental toughness is both a combination of mental conditioning and physical fitness.

No one can argue with the fact that most high-risk occupations are mentally and physically demanding. Moreover, many violent situations are unpredictable and occur without warning. Warriors must be able to handle the sudden and intense demands placed on the body during a crisis. Physical fitness or combat conditioning is the best way to achieve this goal.

Physical fitness is also critical for sports performance. Besides sport specific training, athletes also need to be physically fit. A physically fit athlete is more likely to reach his or her full potential. In most cases, they perform more efficiently and effectively and are less likely to be injured. Finally, athletes who regularly work out are more disciplined and possess greater self-confidence than their unconditioned counterparts

Fitness and Combat Conditioning

If boxers and athletes want to achieve peak performance, they

Tough Enough

must be physically fit. It's that simple. Fitness and conditioning comprises the following three broad components: cardiorespiratory conditioning, muscular/skeletal conditioning, and proper body composition.

The cardiorespiratory system includes the heart, lungs, and circulatory system, which undergo tremendous stress in a high-risk situation. So you're going to have to run, jog, bike, swim, or skip rope to develop sound cardiorespiratory conditioning. Each aerobic workout should last a minimum of 30 minutes and be performed at least four times per week.

The second component of conditioning is muscular/skeletal conditioning. To strengthen your bones and muscles to withstand the rigors of both sport and combat performance, your training must include progressive resistance (weight training). You will also need a stretching program designed to loosen up every muscle group. Stretching on a regular basis will also increase the muscles' range of motion, improve circulation, reduce the possibility of injury and relieve daily stress.

The final component of conditioning is proper body composition: simply, the ratio of fat to lean body tissue. Your diet and training regimen will affect your level or percentage of body fat significantly. A sensible and consistent exercise program accompanied by a healthy and balanced diet will facilitate proper body composition.

Exercise and fitness is not limited to fighters and athletes. Anyone interested in improving their overall health should exercise on a

Chapter 4: Physical Training Mental Toughness

consistent basis. In fact, there are many good reasons why you should exercise on a regular basis. Here are just a few:

1. To increase longevity.
2. To lose excess body weight, which can shorten life.
3. To improve your circulation.
4. To tone and firm muscles and acquire the physical proportions nature intended.
5. To relax from tensions causing undue fatigue and loss of sleep.
6. To stay mentally alert.
7. To improve your metabolism.
8. To improve your immune system.
9. To acquire a more positive outlook through the feeling of good health and well-being.
10. To help maintain a youthful appearance.
11. To get more enjoyment out of life.
12. To improve your memory.
13. To improved posture.
14. To improved self-confidence.
15. To improve sleep.
16. To generate creative thinking.

Nutrition & Supplements for Mental Toughness

One important yet frequently overlooked aspect of mental toughness training is diet and nutrition. In reality, a true diet refers to a lifestyle of eating right.

To begin, 55 percent of daily caloric intake should consist of complex carbohydrates. Carbohydrates, the body's primary source of energy, are found in vegetables, fruits, potatoes, pasta, and all grain products.

Next we have proteins, which are essential for muscle and tissue growth. Poultry, fish, and legumes are excellent sources of low-fat proteins. Since you are involved in peak performance, you will require a greater amount of protein than the average person. Generally speaking, you should consume 1-1.5 grams of protein per pound of lean mass.

Finally, unsaturated fats are vital to proper metabolic function and vitamin absorption and should make up 10 percent of your calories. Don't confuse unsaturated fats with their nasty relatives, saturated fats. Saturated fats, found in ice cream, chocolate, cakes, and so on, are a big NO! Forget them. They will only make you fat and sluggish. Look for natural unsaturated fats in such foods as nuts, seeds, and various grains.

Do not forget to drink plenty of water throughout the day. Water is essential nutrient and it plays a significant role in all bodily processes. Try to drink at least one gallon of water per day!

Vitamins

Nutritional supplements should also be taken to ensure that you are receiving all the necessary vitamins and minerals within your diet. A vitamin is any of various fat-soluble (stored in the body fat) or water-soluble (dissolve in water) organic substances essential for the

Chapter 4: Physical Training Mental Toughness

growth and maintenance of the body.

While a well-balanced diet will ensure that you are taking in the necessary amounts of vitamins, deficiencies can still occur, and they can have a negative effect on your training and overall performance. Be certain to get the following vitamins within your daily diet.

Vitamin A – this fat-soluble vitamin is important for normal cell growth and development. Vitamin A can be found in fish-liver oils, carrots, liver, fortified dairy products, and some yellow and dark green vegetables.

Vitamin D – this fat-soluble vitamin helps build healthy bones and teeth, and it can be obtained from fortified milk, fish, and eggs, and by exposing your body to sunlight.

Vitamin E – this fat-soluble vitamin is used to treat abnormalities of the muscles, red blood cells, liver, and brain. This vitamin can be found in seed oils, especially wheat germ oil, plant leaves, and milk.

Vitamin K – this fat-soluble vitamin is important for blood clotting and preventing hemorrhaging. It can be found in fish oils, liver, egg yolks, tomatoes, and green, leafy vegetables.

Vitamin B1 (Thiamin) – this water-soluble vitamin functions as a coenzyme and is necessary for carbohydrate metabolism and neural activity. Thiamin can be found in meat, yeast, and the bran coat of grains.

Vitamin B2 (Riboflavin) – is the primary growth-promoting factor in the vitamin B complex. It can be found in milk, leafy vegetables, liver, nuts, brewer's yeast, meat, and egg yolks.

Niacin – a component of the vitamin B complex used to treat and prevent pellagra (a disease that includes skin eruptions, nausea, vomiting, nervous system disturbances, and mental deterioration). Niacin can be found in meat, fish, poultry, wheat germ, dairy products, and yeast.

Tough Enough

Vitamin C (Ascorbic Acid) – this water-soluble vitamin prevents scurvy and a variety of dental problems. Vitamin C can be found in citrus fruits, tomatoes, turnips, sweet potatoes, potatoes, and leafy green vegetables.

Supplements

Look at any fitness magazine you'll see hundreds of advertisements for supplements claiming to make you bigger and stronger in the shortest amount of time. With so much on the market, it's hard to choose the best supplements for your conditioning program.

Throughout the years, I have discovered three supplements that are tried and true for gaining lean muscle mass and strength. They include: creatine, glutamine and whey protein. Let take a look at each one.

Creatine

Creatine is a fascinating supplement that can benefit anyone who wants to boost their strength and endurance and build lean muscle mass. Creatine is a tasteless and odorless, white powder that is relatively inexpensive. Creatine mimics some of the effects of anabolic steroids. While results will vary from person to person, it's not uncommon for some people to gain 5 to 10 pounds of lean muscle within a few weeks of intense weight training.

The best time to consume creatine is approximately 1/2 hour before weight training and then right after a workout. Also, be certain to drink plenty of water when taking creatine (at least eight-8 ounce glasses per day). Creatine needs water for cell volumization of the muscle.

Be careful when purchasing creatine. There are some manufacturers who sell impure creatine that can be harmful to your body. Make certain you are ingesting 100% pure creatine. Demand to see the HPLC (high-performance liquid chromatography) test results from whomever you purchased your creatine from. If you purchase creatine that has a strange smell or is yellow in color, return it immediately to the place of purchase and get a full refund.

Glutamine

Next, is Glutamine. Essentially, glutamine is an amino acid produced in the body that plays a vital role in protein synthesis. Despite its abundance in the muscles, glutamine levels can become quickly depleted when your body undergoes intense training. As a matter of fact, studies show that it can take up to approximately six days for Glutamine levels to return to normal after intense weight training sessions. While dosages can often vary from person to person, most people should take 5 grams. It has also been stated that the best time to take glutamine is right before you go to sleep.

Whey Protein

Whey is a high quality protein that is loaded with all the essential amino acids. The benefit to whey protein is that it is rapidly digested and helps quickly repair your muscles following intense training.

As you can imagine, there are numerous brands of whey protein sold on the market at various prices. The good news is whey protein tastes decent and comes in a wide range of flavors, so you will most likely find something that agrees with your palette.

How Much Protein?

There is much debate on the subject of protein consumption for conditioning, muscular development and overall health. Generally speaking, the average healthy adult male should consume approximately 1-1.5 grams of protein per pound of body weight. For

Tough Enough

example, a 175 pound man would consume anywhere from 175 to 262 grams of protein per day. This 1-1.5 protein ratio will help with the following:

- Build muscle mass.
- Maintain muscle tone while losing fat.
- Increase strength.
- Improving both sports and combat performance.

Chapter Five
Mental Training for Mental Toughness

Tough Enough

Mental Training for Mental Toughness

In this chapter, I will be teaching you several cognitive exercises to develop and improve your level of mental toughness. Some of these exercises can also be used as coping tools during the immediate stress and anxiety of a high-performance situation. Let's begin with creative visualization.

Mental Visualization

Through years of research and training, I found mental visualization to be a fascinating subject. Briefly stated, visualization is the formation of mental images to bring about desired goals ranging anywhere from improved lifestyles and health to better job performance and athletic ability. Established research indicates that mental images cause brain activity identical to that produced by an actual experience. Even if the image is unrealistic or logically impossible, the body will still produce a response that stimulates every cell in the body. There is no doubt that visualization can significantly improve mental toughness. To truly reap the benefits, however, you must make certain that your images are clear and strong. In essence, you must feel, taste, smell, and here the visualized scenario.

Visualization for Mental Toughness

Visualization serves many purposes in mental toughness training. As a training aid, visualization improves concentration, selective attention, self-confidence, instrumental aggression and helps maintain motivation during grueling workouts.

In sports, practice and training will only take you so far. In order to maximize your athletic potential, you must learn to use the mind's eye to further enhance your skills and abilities. The same applies to combat performance during extremely dangerous and hostile encounters. For example, visualizing strategic solutions to various high-risk combat scenarios also enhances performance and reduces the possibility of making tactical mistakes.

How to do it

Visualization is a natural and relatively simple exercise. The good news is the more often you use it, the easier it becomes. Effective visualization requires a quiet place, free from distractions, for at least 20 minutes. Turn off your cell phone and tell your partner or roommates that you do not wish to be disturbed. It is vital that you have peace and quiet.

Every visualization session must be undertaken in a relaxed state, the preparatory state for visualization. To attain a state of relaxation, you must first sit in a chair or lie on a couch or bed. If sitting, make certain your back is straight, your arms are uncrossed, and your feet are both on the floor. If lying down, place your arms at your side. You may want to put a pillow under your head.

There are various relaxation exercises you can perform. One of the easiest to learn is the tensing – releasing method. To begin, close your eyes and begin to breathe slowly and deeply for approximately 2 minutes. The next step requires you to tense every muscle in your body all at once. Clench your fists and your feet. Tighten your jaw and facial muscles. Tense your shoulders, chest, back, legs, and buttocks. Hold the tension for approximately 10 seconds then in one concentrated effort, let go and allow the tension to flow out of your body.

Visualization Example

In this section, I am going to show you how to use visualization techniques to improve specific aspects of mental toughness. Here is a good example of what you can do with mental imagery. Let's begin

Chapter 5: Mental Training for Mental Toughness

with improving your training performance.

Training Performance Visualization

Before visualizing your training event, you must first have a clear mental picture of yourself. Begin by closing your eyes and visualizing yourself in a relaxed and peaceful state. Visualize your physical characteristics. Imagine your face. Note your eyes, nose, mouth, and chin. Observe the length and color of your hair. Now, look at your torso and concentrate on your chest and shoulders. See the veins that run up and down your biceps, forearms, and hands. Focus on your quadriceps, hamstrings, calves, and feet. Concentrate on the clarity of the vision. It may be helpful to glance at a picture of yourself occasionally to get a clear image.

Now, visualize yourself in a very serious training environment, maybe at a nearby gym. Visualize your surroundings. For example, envision a large, dingy and well-equipped gym. Feel the dank air against your face, neck and arms. Smell the subtle odor of sweat as you walk past three athletes working out. Listen to the sound of iron plates crashing to the floor. Remember, mental imagery is not limited to the visual. Concentrate on crystallizing this entire scenario. This may require you to run it numerous times in your head to bring it into full focus.

Next, picture yourself performing various weight training exercises. For example, you are now going to perform heavy squats. Envision yourself confidently walk up to the squat rack and load six 45-pound plates on the Olympic bar. See yourself tighten a weight lifting belt around your waist as you approach the bar. Imagine resting the back of your shoulders under the bar while holding it in place with both of your hands. Picture a solid stance with your feet approximately shoulder width apart from each other. Feel the heaviness of the weight and the strain in your muscles as you lift the heavy bar from the rack. Now, visualize the perfect execution of a leg squat – head up, back straight, and your feet flush against the floor. Watch yourself breathe deeply as you slowly lower your body to the squat position. Imagine yourself exploding upward back to the starting position. Experience the sensation of pure confidence as you start another repetition. Continue this mental imagery for each and every repetition in your set.

Now, visualize how you feel after your leg workout. Imagine the distinct soreness in your leg muscles. Feel them cramp and ache from complete exhaustion. Picture how difficult it is to walk up a flight of stairs after training your legs. Experience that priceless feeling of accomplishment and achievement as you amble your way to your car.

Meditation and Mental Toughness

Meditation is a technique whereby the practitioner achieves a state of deep physiological and mental repose. It has been used throughout the centuries by the Indian yogis, Taoists, Buddhists, and the mystics to achieve self-enlightenment. It wasn't until the 60s that Westerners recognize the value of meditation for reducing stress, muscle tension, pulse rate, high blood pressure, and other ailments.

Meditation serves several purposes in mental toughness training. It develops both self-discipline and self-awareness. Meditation also enhances concentration. Through its practice, you learn to eliminate both internal and external distractions from your mind. Believe it or not, meditation also cultivates characteristics of instrumental aggression. Through consistent practice, you can acquire an emotionless state of mind that is essential for high-risk combat operations. Meditation can also be used to clear the warrior's mind after a dangerous and stressful combat event. Stress and anxiety are replaced with inner peace, patience and a state of well-being.

Chapter 5: Mental Training for Mental Toughness

How to do it

Effective meditation requires a quiet environment and freedom from distractions for at least 30 minutes. A quiet and comfortable room will suffice. There is no need to burn incense or decorate your room in an oriental motif. Just keep it plain and simple. Meditation can also be practiced outdoors, as long as the location is quiet and peaceful.

Posture is another important factor. You want to be as comfortable as possible when meditating. There are many different types of meditative postures. The most common is the seated, cross-legged position, where the legs are crossed with the feet under the thighs. The head is balanced and facing forward, the torso is erect, and the hands are placed on the knees. This is by far the most comfortable and unrestricted posture. I do not recommend lying down; you should not be so relaxed that the mind becomes unfocused.

Once you are in a comfortable position, close your eyes and begin to breathe slowly and deeply, in through your nose and out through your mouth. The goal is to relax. The next step is the most difficult. You want to eliminate any thoughts from your mind. The objective is to remain mentally void. Don't let your mind wander or visualize. You want to reach a state of "nothingness." If thoughts or images do enter your mind, don't concentrate on them. Just allow them to drift from your consciousness. Concentrating on "nothing" can be difficult and very frustrating. It becomes easier with constant practice, however. If your schedule permits, meditate every day. If your time is limited, three times a week will suffice. Make sure each session lasts at least 20 minutes.

Remember that results will not come overnight. Like any worthwhile endeavor, meditation requires practice and time.

Controlled Breathing

Controlled breathing is a very useful technique for managing the stress and anxiety associated with a variety of high-performance tasks. This form of tactical breathing can be used by warriors and athletes. However, it's especially helpful for arousal control during intense fighting.

All of us, at one time or another, have experienced the uncontrolled breathing pattern associated with fear or extreme stress. If you recall, it was loud, fast and shallow. Therefore, the objective of controlled breathing is to do the exact opposite. By employing slow and controlled breathing, you will be able to regain control of your emotional state. Deep and steady breathing quickly shifts your mind and body into a more relaxed state, so you can efficiently perform your task or mission during a crisis situation.

How to do it

Initially, controlled breathing should be practiced in a quiet place, free from distractions, for at least 15 minutes. It's best to practice while sitting in a chair or lying on a comfortable couch or bed. If sitting, make certain your back is straight, your arms are uncrossed, and your feet are both on the floor. If lying down, place your arms at your side. You may want to put a pillow under your head.

Next, close your eyes and relax your body. Begin by inhaling deeply and steadily for 4 seconds. Let your lungs fill and expand with air. Hold this for one second and then exhale steadily for 4 seconds. Allow all of the air to expel from your mouth. Repeat this process for a minimum of 15 minutes. Advanced practitioners can also incorporate controlled breathing exercises with mental visualization scenarios. The more you practice controlled breathing, the faster you'll be able to bring about its relaxation response.

Chapter 5: Mental Training for Mental Toughness

Once you master the basics, you can practice controlled breathing during idle times. For example, when you are waiting in a long line or when you are stuck in a traffic jam. However, controlled breathing is best used before, during and after a high-pressure performance situation.

Positive Thinking & Self-Talk

Many people underestimate the power of positive thinking. As a matter of fact, research suggests numerous health benefits from positive and optimistic thinking. Some include:

- Increased longevity
- Greater resistance to illness
- Improved productivity
- Improved self-esteem
- Improved physical well-being
- Reduced risk of heart disease
- Greater coping skills during stressful events

Positive thinking is especially important for mental toughness. In order to effectively overcome adversity, you must possess the self-confidence and personal belief that you can overcome any obstacle or hardship. However, don't confuse positive thinking with arrogance, self-delusion or blind hope. Positive thinking must be predicated on competency. You must, in fact, possess the actual skills and attributes necessary to address your adverse situation.

Positive Self-Talk

Positive thinking is the environment necessary for effective self-talk. Self-talk is the internal dialogue you have with yourself during a stressful performance situation, and it's based on your beliefs, assumptions, and individual perceptions. This internal dialogue is essential to identifying and solving problems during a performance event. In fact, positive self-talk during performance situations improves attention control and will help eliminate self-doubts and false assumptions, which can destroy peak performance.

Positive self-talk is a skill, and like any skill, it takes practice. Here are several techniques that will get you started in the right direction.

- Be self-aware and learn to catch yourself when you are thinking negatively.
- Whenever a negative self-statement is made, quickly replace it with a positive and optimistic one. For example, change "I suck!" to "I love this challenge."
- Interrupt negative self-talk with a positive visual image of yourself (i.e., completing the mission, scoring a touchdown, defeating the enemy, etc.).
- Regularly visualize yourself in positive and favorable situations.
- Intentionally use positive words in your inner dialogues, or when talking with other people.
- Approach every situation or circumstance with favorable expectations.
- Make it a habit to take control of stressful situations.
- Try to associate with people who are positive and upbeat.

Using Cue Words

A cue word is a unique word or personal statement that helps focus your attention on the execution of a skill, instead of its outcome. It is also a very effective thought-stopping technique for halting unwanted thoughts during a crisis.

For example, since the brain can only focus on one thing at a

Chapter 5: Mental Training for Mental Toughness

time, concentrating on a specific cue word is a very effective way of taking your mind off negative thoughts during a performance event. Cue words, however, should be positive, personal and short. They can also include action statements or instructional phrases.

Sample Cue Words or Statements:

- "Attack!"
- "Explode!"
- "Tough!"
- "Dominate!"
- "Shoot!"
- "Fight"
- "Focus!"
- "Relax!"
- "Hit!"
- "Punch!"
- "Move!"
- "Steady!"
- "Power!"
- "Hold on!"
- "Swing!"
- "Jump!"
- "Faster!"
- "In Control!"
- "Ready, Set, Go!"
- "Eye on the Ball!"
- "Crush him!"

Tough Enough

Optical Illusion Exercises

The following exercises are designed to improve your selective attention and concentration skills. Each drawing is an optical illusion that presents one of two different perceptual images.

The goal is to concentrate and focus exclusively on only one perceptual image for a specified period of time. Start off with 15 seconds and progressively work your way up to 5 minutes. Remember, if your attention breaks (and you see the other image), you must start over again. This may sound easy to some, but I assure you that it is not.

- Beginner level – 15 seconds.
- Intermediate level – 30 seconds.
- Skilled level – 90 seconds.
- Advanced level – 3 minutes.
- Mental Mastery level – 5 minutes.

Chapter 5: Mental Training for Mental Toughness

The Rubin Vase

What do you see? Is it a curved vase or two faces looking directly at each other? Concentrate and focus on only one perceptual image.

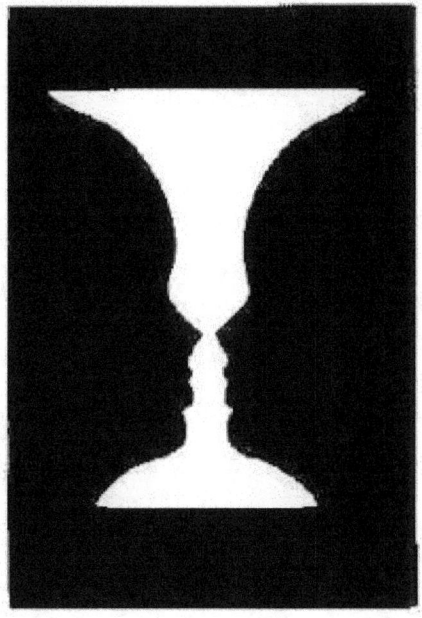

Tough Enough

Young Lady or Old Woman

What do you see? Is it a young lady or old woman? Concentrate and focus on only one perceptual image.

Chapter 5: Mental Training for Mental Toughness

The Face

What do you see? Is it a woman standing next to a tree or a face staring at you? Concentrate and focus on only one perceptual image.

Tough Enough

Woman Reading a Book or Old Man

What do you see? Is it a woman reading a book or the face of an old man? Concentrate and focus on only one perceptual image.

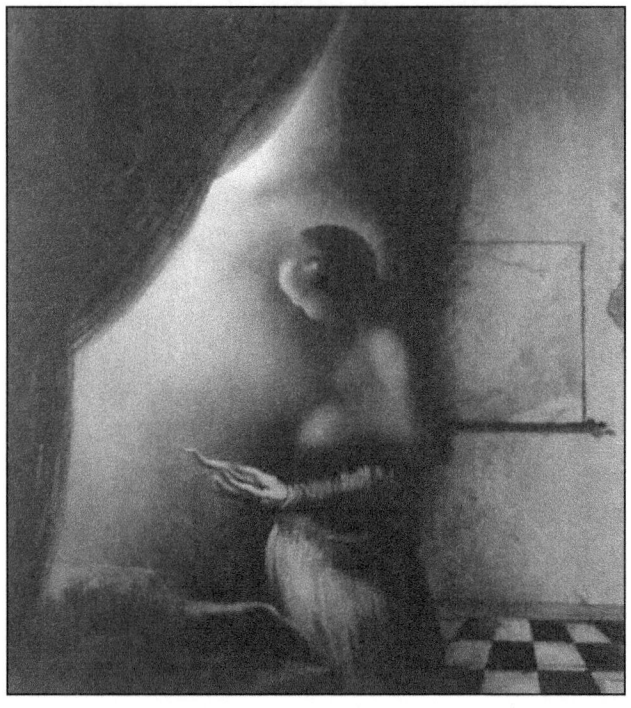

Chapter 5: Mental Training for Mental Toughness

The Devil Face

What do you see? Is it a devil face or a group of women standing in front of their own reflections in a mirror? Concentrate and focus on only one perceptual image.

Bifurcation Training

Bifurcation training is ideal for improving selective attention and mental concentration. This exercise requires the fighter to perform a particular physical performance action while simultaneously executing an unrelated mental task. The physical performance could be anything that involves technical skill and movement (i.e., punching combination, application of defensive skills, etc). The mental task portion of the drill, however, requires you either to solve a mathematical equation or recite a verse or nursery rhyme.

The following bifurcation drills will use a striking combination or "compound attack" as the physical performance action. Let's begin with the pledge drill.

Pledge Drill

This exercise requires that you verbally recite the pledge of allegiance. While you are reciting the pledge your training partner or coach yells, "Go!" and you are to immediately launch a preselected compound attack in the air. The key is to deliver a flurry of full-speed, full-force strikes while continuing to recite the pledge in a calm and controlled manner. It's critical that you do not alter the tone, pitch, volume, or tempo of your voice when delivering your assault.

Nursery Rhyme Drill (beginner level)

This exercise is similar to "the pledge" except that it requires you to verbally recite a simple children's nursery rhyme, such as "Mary Had a Little Lamb" or "Hickory, Dickory, Dock." Once again, while you are reciting the rhyme, your training partner yells, "Go!" and you are to immediately launch a preselected compound attack in the air without disturbing the vocalization of the rhyme. Once again, it's critical not to alter the tonality of your voice when delivering your assault.

Chapter 5: Mental Training for Mental Toughness

Tongue Twister (intermediate level)

The tongue twister is an intermediate-level drill that requires you to slowly and repeatedly recite a tongue twister, such as "She sells seashells on the seashore of Seychelles" or "Peter Piper picked a peck of pickled peppers." While you are reciting this statement, your coach yells, "Go!" and you must immediately launch a preselected compound attack in the air. Once again, it's critical that you do not disturb the vocalization or alter the tone, pitch, volume, or tempo of your voice when delivering your assault.

The Alphabet Drill (advanced level)

The "alphabet" is a more advanced drill. Your objective here is to slowly recite the alphabet backward. At some point during your recitation, your training partner is to yell, "Go!" and you are to immediately launch a preselected compound attack in the air while continuing to recite the alphabet backward. Don't get frustrated with this exercise; it's designed to challenge you.

Sample Compound Attacks

What follows are five compound attacks that can be employed when conducting bifurcation training. A "compound attack" is the logical sequence of two or more techniques thrown in strategic succession. For example, a lead straight punch followed immediately by a rear cross is considered to be a compound attack. There are infinite fighting combinations you can perform during bifurcation training. (For more information about specific fighting techniques, please see the appendix of this book.)

When executing your compound attack, make certain your strikes are delivered with speed, power, and proper form. You can also perform these combinations in front of a mirror, on the heavy bag or the focus mitts.

Tough Enough

> Jab/straight right/jab
>
> Rear uppercut/lead uppercut/rear hook punch
>
> Jab/straight right/lead hook punch/rear hook punch
>
> Rear hook punch/lead hook punch/rear uppercut
>
> Rear hook punch/lead uppercut/rear uppercut/lead hook punch

Opportunity Training

Opportunity training is used during idle times or when a unique situation presents the "opportunity" to practice your mental toughness skills. Here are a few examples:

Insomnia

All of us suffer from insomnia. Insomnia is generally caused by stress and anxiety from a variety of issues and factors, some include relationship and financial problems, job loss, moving, divorce, illness, emotional or physical discomfort, and environmental factors like noise, light, or extreme temperatures.

If you can't sleep, use it as an opportunity to work on your attention control skills. Practice controlled breathing and focus on blocking out the negative and stressful thoughts that are keeping you up. Continue doing this until you fall back asleep.

Delayed Flight

Imagine being stuck on an airplane for 6 hours on the runway. It sounds like hell, and it is. Use this situation as an opportunity to practice your mental visualization skills.

For example, close your eyes and begin visualizing positive and vivid images, such as the plane taking off, the view from the window, the plane landing, and the feelings you will experience when you reach your destination. Keep visualizing these images until your

Chapter 5: Mental Training for Mental Toughness

plane actually takes off.

Crying Baby

Nothing claws at your brain more than a baby screaming on the top of his lungs. Instead of leaving the area, use this as an opportunity to develop your attention control skills. Try to filter out and ignore the high-pitch crying and blood-curdling screams. Direct your attention to something else in your immediate environment. For example, try memorizing lines of a verse during the tantrum. The turmoil around you can work to strengthen both your selective attention and concentration.

Tattoos

Getting tattooed is no picnic. As a matter of fact, it can be downright miserable. Especially, if you are having a lot of work done on a sensitive part of your body, such as the wrist, elbow or ribs.

Initially, getting tattooed might seem exciting, but I can assure you the excitement wears off real fast. The process of being tattooed is painful, boring and mentally draining. A few hours "in the chair" will make you want to scream and rip your hair out.

However, if you must get tattooed, use it as an opportunity to develop your mental resilience and attention control skills. Try to disassociate your mind from the constant pain and irritation of the needle digging relentlessly into your skin. Focus and direct your attention to something else in the room, perhaps a picture on the wall or an object on a table in front of you. Try to maintain this form of attention control for the duration of your tattoo session.

Reading and Research

The intellectual, or academic, aspects of mental toughness training cannot be overstated. You must possess an insatiable

Tough Enough

desire to learn and grow to your full potential. Academic research involves voracious reading. The body of printed materials on mental toughness has grown astronomically.

Try to read anything you can get your hands on. However, don't make the common mistake of passively reading material. Get into the habit of dissecting and noting literature. Strategically sound theories and unique training concepts should be noted and remembered. Books should be read over and over again until practical ideas are intellectually solidified. Finally, always read material with an open mind balanced with healthy skepticism.

Chapter Six
Mental Toughness Programs

Tough Enough

Chapter 6: Mental Toughness Programs

Designing a Mental Toughness Program

We are now going to take all of the knowledge from the previous chapters and put it into action. In this section, I am going to show you how to design a mental toughness training program to suit your personal needs. However, before we begin, you must be certain that your program meets the following criteria.

- **Realistic** – your training should be as real as possible. It should include drills and exercises that replicate real world fighting conditions.

- **Simple** – your training should be easy to put into action. It should not require time-consuming preparation or expensive equipment.

- **Specific** – your training should meet specific training goals. This might be a micro goal, such as improving your instrumental aggression during a particular drill. Avoid the urge to jump from one mental toughness attribute to the next. Instead, devote your attention to one skill at a time.

- **Stressful** – your training should produce one or more of the six types of stressors (i.e., acute emotional stress, mental confusion, mental fatigue, physical fatigue (muscular or aerobic), physical discomfort or pain, and environmental stress).

- **Quantifiable** – you must be able to accurately measure your progress in training. Performance measurement is motivational and helps you stay committed to your goals. It is also useful for identifying methodologies that are not helping you reach your personal objectives.

Sample Mental Toughness Programs

Let me start by saying, there's no single mental toughness program that works for everyone. Since each athlete has different goals and timelines, it's up to you to identify your needs and personalize your training accordingly. The bottom line is, only you can determine what works best for you.

There are many ways to set up a mental toughness training program. In fact, some of you might want to first consult with your coach, trainer or instructor prior to setting up a program and schedule.

How to do it...

What follows are several sample mental toughness programs utilizing both physical and cognitive exercises. Once again, these just serve as examples of what you can do.

STEP 1: IDENTIFY YOUR MICRO-GOAL: For this example, our immediate goal is to develop and improve the attention control attribute.

STEP 2: SELECT YOUR DRILLS: Now, choose from the list of drills that develop this particular mental toughness attribute. In this case, you will choose from the list below:

Physical Drills:

- Impact training
- Medicine ball work
- Proficiency training
- Hip fusing
- Gauntlet drill
- Sparring

Chapter 6: Mental Toughness Programs

- Circle combat
- Heavy bag training
- Elevation drill
- Head hunter drill
- Focus mitt work
- 360-degree blocking
- Sidestepping drill
- Shadowboxing
- Adverse weather training

Mental Drills:

- Visualization
- Meditation
- Controlled breathing
- Bifurcation drills
- Optical illusion exercises
- Reading and research
- Opportunity training

STEP 3: DETERMINE YOUR TRAINING FREQUENCY:
Now, decide how many days per week your schedule permits you to train.

Training Routine Examples

Here are a few sample training routines to get you started. Again, these just serve as examples of what you can do. Remember to be creative and open-minded.

Example 1: Training 2 days per week (mental & physical drills)

Monday– Impact training, Controlled breathing exercises

Tuesday– rest

Wednesday–

Thursday– rest

Friday– Medicine ball work, Sparring, Visualization

Saturday– rest

Sunday – rest

Example 2: Training 3 days per week (mental & physical drills)

Monday– Meditation, Sparring

Tuesday– rest

Wednesday– Visualization, Focus Mitt Training

Thursday– rest

Friday– Impact Training, Sparring, Controlled Breathing

Saturday– rest

Sunday – rest

Example 3: Training 4 days per week (mental & physical drills)

Monday– Optical illusion exercises, Visualization

Tuesday– Hip Fusing, Focus Mitts,

Chapter 6: Mental Toughness Programs

Wednesday– rest

Thursday– Meditation, Controlled Breathing

Friday– Impact Training, Sparring

Saturday– rest

Sunday – rest

Example 4: Training 5 days per week (advanced)

Monday – Elevation Drill, Shadowboxing, Controlled Breathing

Tuesday – Meditation, Heavy Bag Training

Wednesday – rest

Thursday – Sparring, Visualization, Reading and research

Friday – Impact Training, Bifurcation drills

Saturday – Hip Fusing, Controlled Breathing

Sunday – rest

Example 5: Exclusively mental training (3 days)

Monday– Optical illusion exercises, Visualization

Tuesday– rest

Wednesday– Meditation, Controlled Breathing

Thursday– rest

Friday– Reading and research, Opportunity training

Saturday– rest

Sunday – rest

Tough Enough

Example 6: Exclusively physical training (3 days)

Monday – Proficiency training, Medicine ball

Tuesday – rest

Wednesday – Gauntlet drill, Shadowboxing

Thursday – rest

Friday – Sparring, Sidestepping drill

Saturday – rest

Sunday – rest

Mental Toughness Program Tips

1. Try to participate in at least one full-contact training event per week.

2. Commit yourself to only one mental attribute at a time. Devote a least one month to each micro-goal before moving on to another attribute.

3. Try to get at least two visualization and meditation sessions per week. If you can do more, even better.

4. Don't forget to use "opportunity training" throughout the week.

5. Visualization techniques can be performed before, during or after physical training.

6. Meditation sessions can be conducted before or after physical training.

7. Controlled breathing exercises can be conducted before, during or after physical training.

8. Don't be apprehensive to change things around. Remember, nothing is set in stone.

Chapter 6: Mental Toughness Programs

9. Encourage friendly and healthy competition between your training partner.
10. Always maintain a professional attitude when training.
11. Don't expect to be perfect when training.
12. Don't let incorrect habits go uncorrected.
13. Don't get frustrated. Remember, it's a learning process that takes time.
14. Make full use of your rest days. Remember, resting the body is just as important as training. Training intensely day after day will lead to either burnout or injury. The body needs time to recoup and replenish itself from grueling workouts. Remember, there is growth in rest.
15. Since physical fitness goals will vary from person to person, you'll need to incorporate your current fitness/workout regimen (i.e., weight training, cardio, etc.) into your mental toughness program. How you do this, is entirely up to you.

Finding the Right Training Partner

As I discussed earlier, many of these exercises can be performed individually, while others will require the assistance of a training partner, instructor or coach.

A good training partner should motivate, challenge and push you to your limits. He or she doesn't have to share the same goals as you do, but they must be willing to help you reach your full potential. Your training partner or coach should also be somewhat familiar with the various combat drills and equipment. For example, they should know how to hold and manipulate the focus mitts, perform training simulations, and perform full-contact exercises.

While a good training partner can be a major asset, having a bad one can be a major liability. Be exceptionally careful who you choose

Tough Enough

to train with you. When looking for a training partner, try to avoid the following personality types:

- **The Conversationalist** – someone who talks too much and often disrupts the training intensity.
- **The Challenger** – someone who is naturally argumentative and tries to test your knowledge and patience.
- **The Ego Tripper** – someone who will do anything to prove just how tough he is. He usually enjoys full-contact drills and likes to injure others in training.
- **The Insecure One** – someone who is hesitant to participate in training full-contact drills and exercises.
- **The Know-It-All** – someone who thinks he knows anything and everything about mental toughness training.
- **The Dilettante** – someone who doesn't understand the importance of mental toughness training, and doesn't fully commit himself to the program.

Finally, remember that a good training partner or coach is there to evaluate your performance during your workouts. Listen carefully to what he has to say. A good coach, for example, will be brutally honest and tell you what you are doing correctly and what you are doing wrong. Learn to put your ego aside and heed his advice.

Safety When Training

Safety precautions must always be taken when engaged in mental toughness training. Remember, a serious injury can set you back for weeks and even months. Don't make the mistake of letting your ego or laziness get the best of you. Learn to be safety-conscious. Here are a few suggestions to help minimize the possibilities of injury when training:

1. Buy the best training equipment that you can afford.

2. Know the proper way to use training equipment.
3. Regularly inspect your equipment for wear and defects.
4. Avoid ego-driven training partners or coaches.
5. Be especially aware when training with someone of superior size, skill, or experience.
6. Always warm up before training.
7. Drink plenty of water during training sessions to avoid dehydration.
8. Be cautious when performing training drills for the first time.

It's also a good idea to have a first-aid kit nearby. A first-aid kit is intended for both minor and major injuries. The kit should be kept in a well-sealed box away from children. Don't forget to write down the emergency number for your local hospital or medical clinic on the box. Most first-aid kits can be purchased at your local drugstore. Each kit should contain cotton wool and hydrogen peroxide for cleaning cuts, tweezers, scissors, triangular bandages, alcohol swabs, adhesive tape, adhesive bandages, antibiotic ointment, sterile pads, gauze bandages, and elastic bandages for sprains and for elbow and knee injuries.

Avoiding Overtraining & Burnout

Burnout is defined as a negative emotional state acquired by physical overtraining. Some symptoms of burnout include physical illness, boredom, anxiety, disinterest in training, and general sluggish behavior. Whether you are a beginner or expert, you're susceptible to burnout. Here are a few suggestions to help avoid burnout in your training:

- Make your workouts intense but enjoyable.
- Vary your training routine (i.e., hard day/easy day routine).

Tough Enough

- Train to different types of music.
- Pace yourself during your workouts – don't try to do it all in one day.
- Listen to your body- if you don't feel up to training, skip a day.
- Work out in different types of environments.
- Use different types of training equipment.
- Work out with different training partners.
- Keep accurate records of your training routine.
- Vary the intensity of your training throughout your workout.

Keeping Track of Your Training

In order to reap the full benefits of training, you need to keep track of your workouts and monitor your progress. Monitoring your training will give you a wide range of benefits, including:

- Help determine if you are making progress in your training.
- The ability to effectively alter your training program.
- Track your rate of progress,
- Stay interested and motivated.
- Breakthrough performance plateaus.
- Two of the best tools for keeping track of your training progress are: the training journal and video footage. Let's take a look at each one.

The Training Journal

Record keeping is one of the most important and often neglected aspects of mental toughness training. Try to make it a habit to keep

Chapter 6: Mental Toughness Programs

accurate records of your workouts in a personal journal. This type of record keeping is important for some of the following reasons:

1. It will help you monitor your progress.
2. It will keep you organized.
3. It will inspire, motivate and remind you to stick to your goals.
4. It helps prevent potential injuries.
5. It will help you guard against overtraining.
6. If you are learning new skills, it accelerates the learning process.
7. It gives you valuable training information that can be analyzed.
8. It helps you determine which drills, activities, and exercises are unproductive.
9. It helps you determine which activities are helpful and productive.

When making entries in your journal, don't forget to include some of the following important details:

1. The date and time you trained.
2. The mental toughness skill or attribute you are training.
3. The types of drills and exercises you performed.
4. The number or sets, reps you performed for each exercise or drill.
5. The number or rounds and minutes per round you performed for each drill or exercise.
6. The mental toughness skill or attribute you worked on.
7. The feelings you experienced before, during, and after your workout.

Tough Enough

8. Your overall mood.
9. Concerns you have about your current training.
10. Comments, ideas and observations made by your coach, training partner or instructor.

Videotaping

If you really want to actually see your progress, videotape your workouts. The video will provide you with a more accurate picture of what you are doing in your training. You will be able to observe mistakes and recognize your strengths and weaknesses. The video footage will also motivate you to train harder. Remember to date each videotape or video clip; later on you will be able to compare and see marked improvements in your training performance.

Appendix

Tough Enough

Appendix

Boxing Fundamentals

In this section, I am going to teach you the foundational fighting skills required to perform all of the mental toughness drills featured in this book. These basic skills include:

- Boxing stance
- Boxing footwork
- Boxing techniques
- Boxing attributes

Boxing Stance

Any coach worth his salt will agree that a boxer's ability to hit hard begins with his stance. A power puncher must first master a boxing stance that always places his feet, hips and shoulders in the proper position to deliver explosive blows.

For a right handed fighter, this means the following:

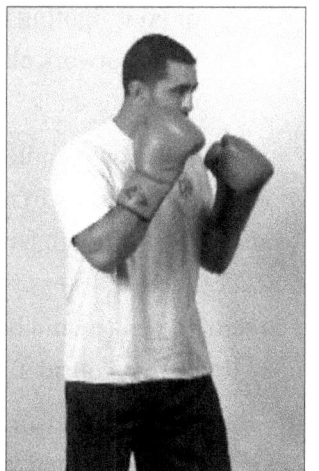

- Left side of your body faces the opponent.
- Left foot extended forward approximately a shoulder width distance from the rear foot.
- Right foot pointing toward the opponent.
- 50% weight distribution on each leg.
- Knees slightly bent.
- Torso is slightly bent.
- Both hands are up and close to your face.

Tough Enough

- Front and rear elbows close to the body and pointing down.
- Shoulders and relaxed but ready.
- Eyes looking forward at the opponent with chin angled down.

Footwork

Footwork is an essential component of boxing because it determines your ability to move and strategically position yourself in the ring. However, many boxers don't realize that footwork also plays two important roles for delivering a knockout punch.

1. **Range Finder** - Footwork facilitates finding your range, which permits you to reach your target at the ideal distance, which will maximize the impact power of your punch.
2. **Power Amplifier** - Footwork functions as a power amplifier for your fighting techniques. Body momentum generated from footwork also acts as a power generator for your punching skills.

Boxing footwork and mobility are one and the same. I define mobility as the ability to move your body quickly and freely, which is accomplished through basic footwork. The safest footwork involves quick, economical steps performed on the balls of your feet, while you remain relaxed and balanced. Keep in mind that balance is your most important consideration.

Basic boxing footwork can be used for both offensive and defensive purposes, and it is structured around four general directions: forward, backward, right, and left.

However, always remember this footwork rule of thumb: Always move the foot closest to the direction you want to go first, and let the other foot follow an equal distance. This will always keep the feet apart from each other and prevent cross-stepping, which can cost you

Appendix

the fight.

Basic Footwork Movements

1. **Moving forward (forward)** - from your fighting stance, first move your front foot forward (approximately 12 inches) and then move your rear foot an equal distance.

2. **Moving backward (backward)** - from your fighting stance, first move your rear foot backward (approximately 12 inches) and then move your front foot an equal distance.

3. **Moving right (sidestep right)** - from your fighting stance, first move your right foot to the right (approximately 12 inches) and then move your left foot an equal distance.

4. **Moving left (sidestep left)** - from your fighting stance, first move your left foot to the left (approximately 12 inches) and then move your right foot an equal distance.

Practice shadowboxing with these four movements for 10 to 15 minutes a day in front of a full-length mirror. In a couple weeks, your footwork should be quick, balanced, and natural.

Circling Right and Left

Circling footwork is a slightly more advanced, where you will use your front leg as a pivot point. This type of movement can also be used defensively to evade an overwhelming combination assault or to counter strike the opponent from a strategic angle. Strategic circling can be performed from either an orthodox or southpaw stance.

1. **Circling left (from a left stance)** - this means you'll be moving your body around the ring in a clockwise direction. From a left stance, step approximately shoulder distance to the left with your left foot. Then use your left leg as a pivot point and wheel your entire right leg to the left (in

the direction of an arc) until the correct boxing stance and positioning is acquired.

2. **Circling right (from a left stance)** - this means you'll be moving your body around the ring in a counter clockwise direction. From a left stance, with your body traveling in the direction of an arc, step approximately shoulder distance to the right with your right foot, then pivot your left foot until the correct stance and positioning is acquired.

When performing circular footwork, remember the footwork rule of thumb still applies: Always move the foot closest to the direction you want to go first, and let the other foot follow an equal distance.

Boxing Techniques

Mastery of basic boxing punches is a necessity for power punching. This includes the following techniques:

- **Left Jab**
- **Straight Right**
- **Left Hook**
- **Right Hook**
- **Left Uppercut**
- **Right Uppercut**

Appendix

The Jab

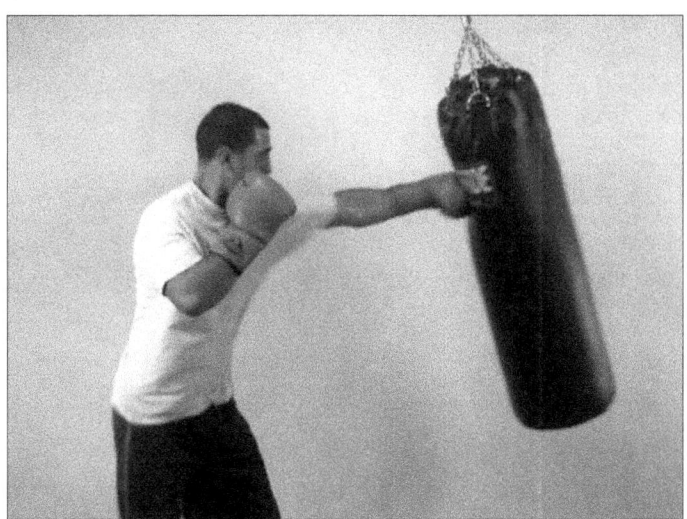

The jab is a foundation technique for boxers and mixed martial artists. This punch is thrown from your front hand and it has a quick snap when delivered.

1. Start off in a fighting stance with both of your hands held up in the guard position. Remember to keep both of your fists lightly clenched with both of your elbows pointing to the ground.
2. To perform the punch, simultaneously step forward and snap your front arm out.
3. Remember to turn your fist so it lands in a horizontal position.
4. When delivering the punch, remember not to lock out your arm, as this will have a "pushing effect".
5. Quickly retract your arm back to the starting position.

Straight Right

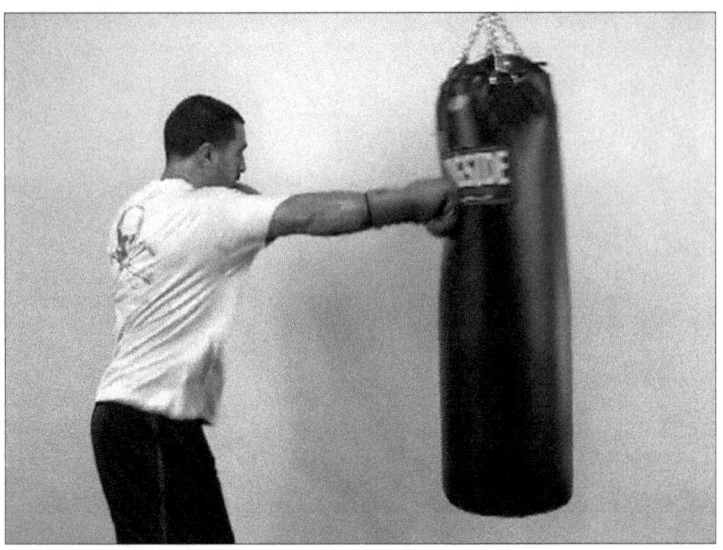

The straight right is considered the heavy artillery of punches and it's thrown from your rear arm. To execute the punch, perform the following steps:

1. Begin from the fighting stance.
2. Quickly twist your rear hips and shoulders forward as you snap your rear arm. Proper weight transfer is of paramount importance. You must shift your weight from your rear foot to your lead leg as you throw the punch.
3. Turn your fist so it lands in a horizontal position.
4. Avoid overextending the blow or exposing your chin during its execution.
5. Don't lock out your arm when throwing the punch. Let punch sink in before retracting it to the starting position.

Appendix

Hook Punch

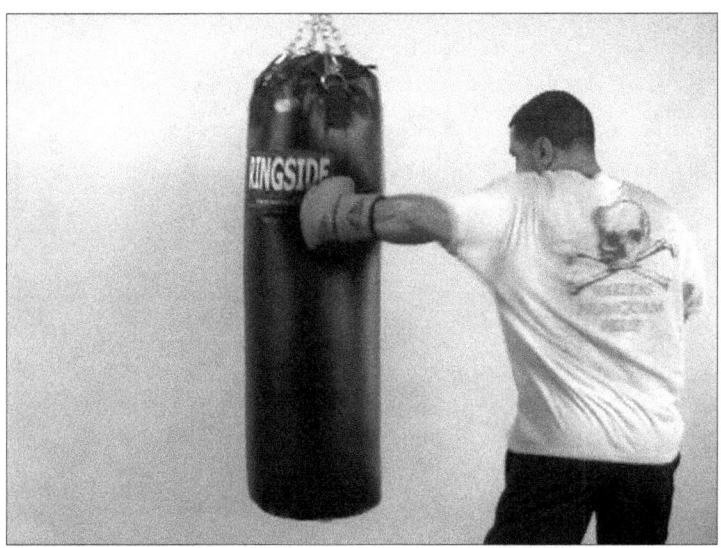

The hook is another devastating punch that's also one of the most difficult to master. This punch can be performed from either your front or rear hand and it can be thrown at both high and low targets.

To perform either the lead or rear hook punch, follow these steps:

1. Start in a fighting stance.
2. Quickly and smoothly, raise your elbow up so that your arm is parallel to the ground while simultaneously torquing your shoulder, hip, and foot into the target.
3. When delivering the punch, be certain your arm is bent at least ninety degrees and that your wrist and forearm are kept straight throughout the movement.
4. Your fist is positioned vertically and your elbow should be locked when contact is made with the opponent.
5. Return back to the starting position.

Tough Enough

Uppercut Punch

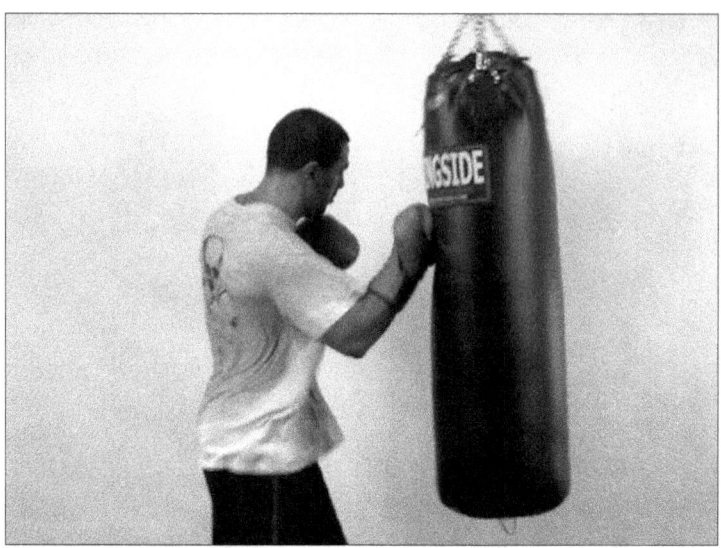

The uppercut is a another powerful punch that can also be delivered from both the lead and rear arm. To perform the technique, follow these steps:

1. Begin from the fighting stance.
2. Next, drop your shoulder and bend your knees.
3. Quickly, lift up and drive your fist upward and into the target.
4. Your palm should be facing you when contact is made with the opponent. To avoid any possible injury, keep your wrists straight.
5. Make certain that the punch has a tight arc and that you avoid any and all "winding up" motions. A properly executed uppercut should be a tight punch and should feel like an explosive jolt.
6. Return back to the fighting stance.

Appendix

Boxing Attributes

For a boxer to be effective in the ring, he or she must possess certain basic fighting attributes. Attributes are both physical and mental qualities that maximize your fighting skills.

For example, speed, power, timing, non telegraphic movement, rhythm, coordination, accuracy, balance, and mental toughness are just a few boxing attributes that must be present if any boxer is to be effective in the ring.

Let's explore a few attributes necessary for boxing: speed, power, timing, balance, and non telegraphic movement.

Speed

You need to be fast. While some athletes are blessed with great speed, the good news is that with proper training you can obtain it rather quickly. In my book Speed Boxing Secrets, I covered in great detail the importance of boxing speed training. Speed development for boxing is actually comprised of two training components:

- Visual reflexes and recognition speed
- Movement speed

Each link in the speed chain represents a particular component or micro-attribute of speed that should be trained and developed to maximize your speed performance in the ring..

Power

Power refers to the amount of impact force you can generate when hitting your opponent. Fortunately, the power of your punch is not necessarily predicated on your size and strength. A relatively small person can generate devastating knockout power if he or she follows the training principles outlined in this book.

Timing

Timing refers to your ability to execute a boxing technique at the optimum moment. There are two types of timing: defensive and offensive. Defensive timing is the time between the opponent's punch and your defensive response to that attack. Offensive timing is the time between your recognition of a target opening and your offensive response to that opening.

Balance

Effectively knockout power requires substantial follow-through while maintaining your balance. Balance is your ability to maintain equilibrium while stationary or moving. You can maintain perfect balance only through controlling your center of gravity, mastering boxing mechanics, and maintaining proper skeletal alignment.

Non Telegraphic Movement

The element of surprise is an invaluable tool in boxing. Successfully landing a knockout blow requires that you don't forewarn your opponent of your intentions. Clenching your teeth, widening your eyes, cocking your fist, and tensing your neck or shoulders are just a few common telegraphic cues that will negate the element of surprise.

One of the best ways to prevent telegraphic movement is to maintain a poker face prior to executing your punch. Make it a habit to always avoid any and all facial expressions when working out in the gym and fighting in the ring.

Glossary

A

accuracy—The precise or exact projection of force. Accuracy is also defined as the ability to execute a combative movement with precision and exactness.

adaptability—The ability to physically and psychologically adjust to new or different conditions or circumstances of combat.

advanced first-strike tools—Offensive techniques that are specifically used when confronted with multiple opponents.

aerobic exercise—Literally, "with air." Exercise that elevates the heart rate to a training level for a prolonged period of time, usually 30 minutes.

affective preparedness – One of the three components of preparedness. Affective preparedness means being emotionally, philosophically, and spiritually prepared for the strains of combat. See cognitive preparedness and psychomotor preparedness.

aggression—Hostile and injurious behavior directed toward a person.

aggressive response—One of the three possible counters when assaulted by a grab, choke, or hold from a standing position. Aggressive response requires you to counter the enemy with destructive blows and strikes. See moderate response and passive response.

aggressive hand positioning—Placement of hands so as to imply aggressive or hostile intentions.

agility—An attribute of combat. One's ability to move his or her body quickly and gracefully.

amalgamation—A scientific process of uniting or merging.

ambidextrous—The ability to perform with equal facility on both the right and left sides of the body.

anabolic steroids – synthetic chemical compounds that resemble the male sex hormone testosterone. This performance-enhancing drug is known to increase lean muscle mass, strength, and endurance.

analysis and integration—One of the five elements of CFA's mental component. This is the painstaking process of breaking down various elements, concepts, sciences, and disciplines into their atomic parts, and then methodically and strategically analyzing, experimenting, and drastically modifying the information so that it fulfills three combative requirements: efficiency, effectiveness, and safety. Only then is it finally integrated into the CFA system.

anatomical striking targets—The various anatomical body targets that can be struck and which are especially vulnerable to potential harm. They include: the eyes, temple, nose, chin, back of neck, front of neck, solar plexus, ribs, groin, thighs, knees, shins, and instep.

anchoring – The strategic process of trapping the assailant's neck or limb in order to control the range of engagement during razing.

assailant—A person who threatens or attacks another person.

assault—The threat or willful attempt to inflict injury upon the person of another.

assault and battery—The unlawful touching of another person without justification.

assessment—The process of rapidly gathering, analyzing, and accurately evaluating information in terms of threat and danger. You can assess people, places, actions, and objects.

attack—Offensive action designed to physically control, injure, or kill another person.

Glossary

attack by combination (ABC) - One of the five methods of attack. See compound attack.

attack by drawing (ABD) - One of the five methods of attack. A method of attack predicated on counterattack.

attitude—One of the three factors that determine who wins a street fight. Attitude means being emotionally, philosophically, and spiritually liberated from societal and religious mores. See skills and knowledge.

attributes of combat—The physical, mental, and spiritual qualities that enhance combat skills and tactics.

awareness—Perception or knowledge of people, places, actions, and objects. (In CFA, there are three categories of tactical awareness: criminal awareness, situational awareness, and self-awareness.)

B

balance—One's ability to maintain equilibrium while stationary or moving.

blading the body—Strategically positioning your body at a 45-degree angle.

blitz and disengage—A style of sparring whereby a fighter moves into a range of combat, unleashes a strategic compound attack, and then quickly disengages to a safe distance. Of all sparring methodologies, the blitz and disengage most closely resembles a real street fight.

block—A defensive tool designed to intercept the assailant's attack by placing a non-vital target between the assailant's strike and your vital body target.

body composition—The ratio of fat to lean body tissue.

body language—Nonverbal communication through posture,

gestures, and facial expressions.

body mechanics—Technically precise body movement during the execution of a body weapon, defensive technique, or other fighting maneuver.

body tackle – A tackle that occurs when your opponent haphazardly rushes forward and plows his body into yours.

body weapon—Also known as a tool, one of the various body parts that can be used to strike or otherwise injure or kill a criminal assailant.

burn out—A negative emotional state acquired by physically over- training. Some symptoms include: illness, boredom, anxiety, disinterest in training, and general sluggishness.

C

cadence—Coordinating tempo and rhythm to establish a timing pattern of movement.

cardiorespiratory conditioning—The component of physical fitness that deals with the heart, lungs, and circulatory system.

centerline—An imaginary vertical line that divides your body in half and which contains many of your vital anatomical targets.

choke holds—Holds that impair the flow of blood or oxygen to the brain.

circular movements—Movements that follow the direction of a curve.

close-quarter combat—One of the three ranges of knife and bludgeon combat. At this distance, you can strike, slash, or stab your assailant with a variety of close-quarter techniques.

cognitive development—One of the five elements of CFA's mental

Glossary

component. The process of developing and enhancing your fighting skills through specific mental exercises and techniques. See analysis and integration, killer instinct, philosophy, and strategic/tactical development.

cognitive exercises—Various mental exercises used to enhance fighting skills and tactics.

cognitive preparedness – One of the three components of preparedness. Cognitive preparedness means being equipped with the strategic concepts, principles, and general knowledge of combat. See affective preparedness and psychomotor preparedness.

combat-oriented training—Training that is specifically related to the harsh realities of both armed and unarmed combat. See ritual-oriented training and sport-oriented training.

combative arts—The various arts of war. See martial arts.

combative attributes—See attributes of combat.

combative fitness—A state characterized by cardiorespiratory and muscular/skeletal conditioning, as well as proper body composition.

combative mentality—Also known as the killer instinct, this is a combative state of mind necessary for fighting. See killer instinct.

combat ranges—The various ranges of unarmed combat.

combative utility—The quality of condition of being combatively useful.

combination(s)—See compound attack.

common peroneal nerve—A pressure point area located approximately four to six inches above the knee on the midline of the outside of the thigh.

composure—A combative attribute. Composure is a quiet and focused mind-set that enables you to acquire your combative agenda.

compound attack—One of the five conventional methods of attack. Two or more body weapons launched in strategic succession whereby the fighter overwhelms his assailant with a flurry of full speed, full-force blows.

conditioning training—A CFA training methodology requiring the practitioner to deliver a variety of offensive and defensive combinations for a 4-minute period. See proficiency training and street training.

contact evasion—Physically moving or manipulating your body to avoid being tackled by the adversary.

Contemporary Fighting Arts—A modern martial art and self-defense system made up of three parts: physical, mental, and spiritual.

conventional ground-fighting tools—Specific ground-fighting techniques designed to control, restrain, and temporarily incapacitate your adversary. Some conventional ground fighting tactics include: submission holds, locks, certain choking techniques, and specific striking techniques.

coordination—A physical attribute characterized by the ability to perform a technique or movement with efficiency, balance, and accuracy.

counterattack—Offensive action made to counter an assailant's initial attack.

courage—A combative attribute. The state of mind and spirit that enables a fighter to face danger and vicissitudes with confidence, resolution, and bravery.

creatine monohydrate—A tasteless and odorless white powder that mimics some of the effects of anabolic steroids. Creatine is a safe body-building product that can benefit anyone who wants to increase their strength, endurance, and lean muscle mass.

Glossary

criminal awareness—One of the three categories of CFA awareness. It involves a general understanding and knowledge of the nature and dynamics of a criminal's motivations, mentalities, methods, and capabilities to perpetrate violent crime. See situational awareness and self-awareness.

criminal justice—The study of criminal law and the procedures associated with its enforcement.

criminology—The scientific study of crime and criminals.

cross-stepping—The process of crossing one foot in front of or behind the other when moving.

crushing tactics—Nuclear grappling-range techniques designed to crush the assailant's anatomical targets.

D

deadly force—Weapons or techniques that may result in unconsciousness, permanent disfigurement, or death.

deception—A combative attribute. A stratagem whereby you delude your assailant.

decisiveness—A combative attribute. The ability to follow a tactical course of action that is unwavering and focused.

defense—The ability to strategically thwart an assailant's attack (armed or unarmed).

defensive flow—A progression of continuous defensive responses.

defensive mentality—A defensive mind-set.

defensive reaction time—The elapsed time between an assailant's physical attack and your defensive response to that attack. See offensive reaction time.

demeanor—A person's outward behavior. One of the essential

factors to consider when assessing a threatening individual.

diet—A lifestyle of healthy eating.

disingenuous vocalization—The strategic and deceptive utilization of words to successfully launch a preemptive strike at your adversary.

distancing—The ability to quickly understand spatial relationships and how they relate to combat.

distractionary tactics—Various verbal and physical tactics designed to distract your adversary.

double-end bag—A small leather ball hung from the ceiling and anchored to the floor with bungee cord. It helps develop striking accuracy, speed, timing, eye-hand coordination, footwork and overall defensive skills.

double-leg takedown—A takedown that occurs when your opponent shoots for both of your legs to force you to the ground.

E

ectomorph—One of the three somatotypes. A body type characterized by a high degree of slenderness, angularity, and fragility. See endomorph and mesomorph.

effectiveness—One of the three criteria for a CFA body weapon, technique, tactic, or maneuver. It means the ability to produce a desired effect. See efficiency and safety.

efficiency—One of the three criteria for a CFA body weapon, technique, tactic, or maneuver. It means the ability to reach an objective quickly and economically. See effectiveness and safety.

emotionless—A combative attribute. Being temporarily devoid of human feeling.

Glossary

endomorph—One of the three somatotypes. A body type characterized by a high degree of roundness, softness, and body fat. See ectomorph and mesomorph.

evasion—A defensive maneuver that allows you to strategically maneuver your body away from the assailant's strike.

evasive sidestepping—Evasive footwork where the practitioner moves to either the right or left side.

evasiveness—A combative attribute. The ability to avoid threat or danger.

excessive force—An amount of force that exceeds the need for a particular event and is unjustified in the eyes of the law.

experimentation—The painstaking process of testing a combative hypothesis or theory.

explosiveness—A combative attribute that is characterized by a sudden outburst of violent energy.

F

fear—A strong and unpleasant emotion caused by the anticipation or awareness of threat or danger. There are three stages of fear in order of intensity: fright, panic, and terror. See fright, panic, and terror.

feeder—A skilled technician who manipulates the focus mitts.

femoral nerve—A pressure point area located approximately 6 inches above the knee on the inside of the thigh.

fighting stance—Any one of the stances used in CFA's system. A strategic posture you can assume when face-to-face with an unarmed assailant(s). The fighting stance is generally used after you have launched your first-strike tool.

Tough Enough

fight-or-flight syndrome—A response of the sympathetic nervous system to a fearful and threatening situation, during which it prepares your body to either fight or flee from the perceived danger.

finesse—A combative attribute. The ability to skillfully execute a movement or a series of movements with grace and refinement.

first strike—Proactive force used to interrupt the initial stages of an assault before it becomes a self-defense situation.

first-strike principle—A CFA principle that states that when physical danger is imminent and you have no other tactical option but to fight back, you should strike first, strike fast, and strike with authority and keep the pressure on.

first-strike stance—One of the stances used in CFA's system. A strategic posture used prior to initiating a first strike.

first-strike tools—Specific offensive tools designed to initiate a preemptive strike against your adversary.

fisted blows – Hand blows delivered with a clenched fist.

five tactical options – The five strategic responses you can make in a self-defense situation, listed in order of increasing level of resistance: comply, escape, de-escalate, assert, and fight back.

flexibility—The muscles' ability to move through maximum natural ranges. See muscular/skeletal conditioning.

focus mitts—Durable leather hand mitts used to develop and sharpen offensive and defensive skills.

footwork—Quick, economical steps performed on the balls of the feet while you are relaxed, alert, and balanced. Footwork is structured around four general movements: forward, backward, right, and left.

fractal tool—Offensive or defensive tools that can be used in more than one combat range.

fright—The first stage of fear; quick and sudden fear. See panic and terror.

full Beat – One of the four beat classifications in the Widow Maker Program. The full beat strike has a complete initiation and retraction phase.

G

going postal - a slang term referring to a person who suddenly and unexpectedly attacks you with an explosive and frenzied flurry of blows. Also known as postal attack.

grappling range—One of the three ranges of unarmed combat. Grappling range is the closest distance of unarmed combat from which you can employ a wide variety of close-quarter tools and techniques. The grappling range of unarmed combat is also divided into two planes: vertical (standing) and horizontal (ground fighting). See kicking range and punching range.

grappling-range tools—The various body tools and techniques that are employed in the grappling range of unarmed combat, including head butts; biting, tearing, clawing, crushing, and gouging tactics; foot stomps, horizontal, vertical, and diagonal elbow strikes, vertical and diagonal knee strikes, chokes, strangles, joint locks, and holds. See punching range tools and kicking range tools.

ground fighting—Also known as the horizontal grappling plane, this is fighting that takes place on the ground.

guard—Also known as the hand guard, this refers to a fighter's hand positioning.

guard position—Also known as leg guard or scissors hold, this is a ground-fighting position in which a fighter is on his back holding his opponent between his legs.

H

half beat – One of the four beat classifications in the Widow

Maker Program. The half beat strike is delivered through the retraction phase of the proceeding strike.

hand immobilization attack (HIA) - One of the five methods of attack. A method of attack whereby the practitioner traps his opponent's limb or limbs in order to execute an offense attack of his own.

hand positioning—See guard.

hand wraps—Long strips of cotton that are wrapped around the hands and wrists for greater protection.

haymaker—A wild and telegraphed swing of the arms executed by an unskilled fighter.

head-hunter—A fighter who primarily attacks the head.

heavy bag—A large cylindrical bag used to develop kicking, punching, or striking power.

high-line kick—One of the two different classifications of a kick. A kick that is directed to targets above an assailant's waist level. See low-line kick.

hip fusing—A full-contact drill that teaches a fighter to "stand his ground" and overcome the fear of exchanging blows with a stronger opponent. This exercise is performed by connecting two fighters with a 3-foot chain, forcing them to fight in the punching range of unarmed combat.

histrionics—The field of theatrics or acting.

hook kick—A circular kick that can be delivered in both kicking and punching ranges.

hook punch—A circular punch that can be delivered in both the punching and grappling ranges.

I

Glossary

impact power—Destructive force generated by mass and velocity.

impact training—A training exercise that develops pain tolerance.

incapacitate—To disable an assailant by rendering him unconscious or damaging his bones, joints, or organs.

initiative—Making the first offensive move in combat.

inside position—The area between the opponent's arms, where he has the greatest amount of control.

intent—One of the essential factors to consider when assessing a threatening individual. The assailant's purpose or motive. See demeanor, positioning, range, and weapon capability.

intuition—The innate ability to know or sense something without the use of rational thought.

J

jeet kune do (JKD) - "Way of the intercepting fist." Bruce Lee's approach to the martial arts, which includes his innovative concepts, theories, methodologies, and philosophies.

jersey Pull - Strategically pulling the assailant's shirt or jacket over his head as he disengages from the clinch position.

joint lock—A grappling-range technique that immobilizes the assailant's joint.

K

kick—A sudden, forceful strike with the foot.

kicking range—One of the three ranges of unarmed combat. Kicking range is the furthest distance of unarmed combat wherein you use your legs to strike an assailant. See grappling range and punching range.

kicking-range tools—The various body weapons employed in the kicking range of unarmed combat, including side kicks, push kicks, hook kicks, and vertical kicks.

killer instinct—A cold, primal mentality that surges to your consciousness and turns you into a vicious fighter.

kinesics—The study of nonlinguistic body movement communications. (For example, eye movement, shrugs, or facial gestures.)

kinesiology—The study of principles and mechanics of human movement.

kinesthetic perception—The ability to accurately feel your body during the execution of a particular movement.

knowledge—One of the three factors that determine who will win a street fight. Knowledge means knowing and understanding how to fight. See skills and attitude.

L

lead side -The side of the body that faces an assailant.

leg guard—See guard position.

linear movement—Movements that follow the path of a straight line.

low-maintenance tool—Offensive and defensive tools that require the least amount of training and practice to maintain proficiency. Low maintenance tools generally do not require preliminary stretching.

low-line kick—One of the two different classifications of a kick. A kick that is directed to targets below the assailant's waist level. (See high-line kick.)

lock—See joint lock.

M

maneuver—To manipulate into a strategically desired position.

MAP—An acronym that stands for moderate, aggressive, passive. MAP provides the practitioner with three possible responses to various grabs, chokes, and holds that occur from a standing position. See aggressive response, moderate response, and passive response.

martial arts—The "arts of war."

masking—The process of concealing your true feelings from your opponent by manipulating and managing your body language.

mechanics—(See body mechanics.)

mental attributes—The various cognitive qualities that enhance your fighting skills.

mental component—One of the three vital components of the CFA system. The mental component includes the cerebral aspects of fighting including the killer instinct, strategic and tactical development, analysis and integration, philosophy, and cognitive development. See physical component and spiritual component.

mesomorph—One of the three somatotypes. A body type classified by a high degree of muscularity and strength. The mesomorph possesses the ideal physique for unarmed combat. See ectomorph and endomorph.

mobility—A combative attribute. The ability to move your body quickly and freely while balanced. See footwork.

moderate response—One of the three possible counters when assaulted by a grab, choke, or hold from a standing position. Moderate response requires you to counter your opponent with a control and restraint (submission hold). See aggressive response and passive response.

modern martial art—A pragmatic combat art that has evolved to meet the demands and characteristics of the present time.

mounted position—A dominant ground-fighting position where a fighter straddles his opponent.

muscular endurance—The muscles' ability to perform the same motion or task repeatedly for a prolonged period of time.

muscular flexibility—The muscles' ability to move through maximum natural ranges.

muscular strength—The maximum force that can be exerted by a particular muscle or muscle group against resistance.

muscular/skeletal conditioning—An element of physical fitness that entails muscular strength, endurance, and flexibility.

N

naked choke—A throat choke executed from the chest to back position. This secure choke is executed with two hands and it can be performed while standing, kneeling, and ground fighting with the opponent.

neck crush – A powerful pain compliance technique used when the adversary buries his head in your chest to avoid being razed.

neutralize—See incapacitate.

neutral zone—The distance outside the kicking range at which neither the practitioner nor the assailant can touch the other.

nonaggressive physiology—Strategic body language used prior to initiating a first strike.

nontelegraphic movement—Body mechanics or movements that do not inform an assailant of your intentions.

nuclear ground-fighting tools—Specific grappling range tools designed to inflict immediate and irreversible damage. Nuclear tools and tactics include biting tactics, tearing tactics, crushing tactics, continuous choking tactics, gouging techniques, raking tactics, and all striking techniques.

O

offense—The armed and unarmed means and methods of attacking a criminal assailant.

offensive flow—Continuous offensive movements (kicks, blows, and strikes) with unbroken continuity that ultimately neutralize or terminate the opponent. See compound attack.

offensive reaction time—The elapsed time between target selection and target impaction.

one-mindedness—A state of deep concentration wherein you are free from all distractions (internal and external).

ostrich defense—One of the biggest mistakes one can make when defending against an opponent. This is when the practitioner looks away from that which he fears (punches, kicks, and strikes). His mentality is, "If I can't see it, it can't hurt me."

P

pain tolerance—Your ability to physically and psychologically withstand pain.

panic—The second stage of fear; overpowering fear. See fright and terror.

parry—A defensive technique: a quick, forceful slap that redirects an assailant's linear attack. There are two types of parries: horizontal and vertical.

passive response—One of the three possible counters when

assaulted by a grab, choke, or hold from a standing position. Passive response requires you to nullify the assault without injuring your adversary. See aggressive response and moderate response.

patience—A combative attribute. The ability to endure and tolerate difficulty.

perception—Interpretation of vital information acquired from your senses when faced with a potentially threatening situation.

philosophical resolution—The act of analyzing and answering various questions concerning the use of violence in defense of yourself and others.

philosophy—One of the five aspects of CFA's mental component. A deep state of introspection whereby you methodically resolve critical questions concerning the use of force in defense of yourself or others.

physical attributes—The numerous physical qualities that enhance your combative skills and abilities.

physical component—One of the three vital components of the CFA system. The physical component includes the physical aspects of fighting, such as physical fitness, weapon/technique mastery, and combative attributes. See mental component and spiritual component.

physical conditioning—See combative fitness.

physical fitness—See combative fitness.

positional asphyxia—The arrangement, placement, or positioning of your opponent's body in such a way as to interrupt your breathing and cause unconsciousness or possibly death.

positioning—The spatial relationship of the assailant to the assailed person in terms of target exposure, escape, angle of attack, and various other strategic considerations.

Glossary

postal attack - see going postal.

power—A physical attribute of armed and unarmed combat. The amount of force you can generate when striking an anatomical target.

power generators—Specific points on your body that generate impact power. There are three anatomical power generators: shoulders, hips, and feet.

precision—See accuracy.

preemptive strike—See first strike.

premise—An axiom, concept, rule, or any other valid reason to modify or go beyond that which has been established.

preparedness—A state of being ready for combat. There are three components of preparedness: affective preparedness, cognitive preparedness, and psychomotor preparedness.

probable reaction dynamics - The opponent's anticipated or predicted movements or actions during both armed and unarmed combat.

proficiency training—A CFA training methodology requiring the practitioner to execute a specific body weapon, technique, maneuver, or tactic over and over for a prescribed number of repetitions. See conditioning training and street training.

progressive indirect attack (PIA) - One of the five methods of attack. A progressive method of attack whereby the initial tool or technique is designed to set the opponent up for follow-up blows.

proxemics—The study of the nature and effect of man's personal space.

proximity—The ability to maintain a strategically safe distance from a threatening individual.

pseudospeciation—A combative attribute. The tendency to assign subhuman and inferior qualities to a threatening assailant.

psychological conditioning—The process of conditioning the mind for the horrors and rigors of real combat.

psychomotor preparedness—One of the three components of preparedness. Psychomotor preparedness means possessing all of the physical skills and attributes necessary to defeat a formidable adversary. See affective preparedness and cognitive preparedness.

punch—A quick, forceful strike of the fists.

punching range—One of the three ranges of unarmed combat. Punching range is the mid range of unarmed combat from which the fighter uses his hands to strike his assailant. See kicking range and grappling range.

punching-range tools—The various body weapons that are employed in the punching range of unarmed combat, including finger jabs, palm-heel strikes, rear cross, knife-hand strikes, horizontal and shovel hooks, uppercuts, and hammer-fist strikes. See grappling-range tools and kicking-range tools.

Q

qualities of combat—See attributes of combat.

quarter beat - One of the four beat classifications of the Widow Maker Program. Quarter beat strikes never break contact with the assailant's face. Quarter beat strikes are primarily responsible for creating the psychological panic and trauma when Razing.

R

range—The spatial relationship between a fighter and a threatening assailant.

range deficiency—The inability to effectively fight and defend in all ranges of combat (armed and unarmed).

Glossary

range manipulation—A combative attribute. The strategic manipulation of combat ranges.

range proficiency—A combative attribute. The ability to effectively fight and defend in all ranges of combat (armed and unarmed).

ranges of engagement—See combat ranges.

ranges of unarmed combat—The three distances (kicking range, punching range, and grappling range) a fighter might physically engage with an assailant while involved in unarmed combat.

raze – To level, demolish or obliterate.

razer – One who performs the Razing methodology.

razing – The second phase of the Widow Maker Program. A series of vicious close quarter techniques designed to physically and psychologically extirpate a criminal attacker.

razing amplifier - a technique, tactic or procedure that magnifies the destructiveness of your razing technique.

reaction dynamics—see probable reaction dynamics.

reaction time—The elapsed time between a stimulus and the response to that particular stimulus. See offensive reaction time and defensive reaction time.

rear cross—A straight punch delivered from the rear hand that crosses from right to left (if in a left stance) or left to right (if in a right stance).

rear side—The side of the body furthest from the assailant. See lead side.

reasonable force—That degree of force which is not excessive for a particular event and which is appropriate in protecting yourself or others.

refinement—The strategic and methodical process of improving or perfecting.

relocation principle—Also known as relocating, this is a street-fighting tactic that requires you to immediately move to a new location (usually by flanking your adversary) after delivering a compound attack.

repetition—Performing a single movement, exercise, strike, or action continuously for a specific period.

research—A scientific investigation or inquiry.

rhythm—Movements characterized by the natural ebb and flow of related elements.

ritual-oriented training—Formalized training that is conducted without intrinsic purpose. See combat-oriented training and sport-oriented training.

S

safety—One of the three criteria for a CFA body weapon, technique, maneuver, or tactic. It means that the tool, technique, maneuver or tactic provides the least amount of danger and risk for the practitioner. See efficiency and effectiveness.

scissors hold—See guard position.

scorching – Quickly and inconspicuously applying oleoresin capsicum (hot pepper extract) on your fingertips and then razing your adversary.

self-awareness—One of the three categories of CFA awareness. Knowing and understanding yourself. This includes aspects of yourself which may provoke criminal violence and which will promote a proper and strong reaction to an attack. See criminal awareness and situational awareness.

Glossary

self-confidence—Having trust and faith in yourself.

self-enlightenment—The state of knowing your capabilities, limitations, character traits, feelings, general attributes, and motivations. See self-awareness.

set—A term used to describe a grouping of repetitions.

shadow fighting—A CFA training exercise used to develop and refine your tools, techniques, and attributes of armed and unarmed combat.

sharking – A counter attack technique that is used when your adversary grabs your razing hand.

shielding wedge - a defensive maneuver used to counter an unarmed postal attack.

simple direct attack (SDA) - One of the five methods of attack. A method of attack whereby the practitioner delivers a solitary offenses tool or technique. It may involve a series of discrete probes or one swift, powerful strike aimed at terminating the encounter.

situational awareness—One of the three categories of CFA awareness. A state of being totally alert to your immediate surroundings, including people, places, objects, and actions. (See criminal awareness and self-awareness.)

skeletal alignment—The proper alignment or arrangement of your body. Skeletal alignment maximizes the structural integrity of striking tools.

skills—One of the three factors that determine who will win a street fight. Skills refers to psychomotor proficiency with the tools and techniques of combat. See Attitude and Knowledge.

slipping—A defensive maneuver that permits you to avoid an assailant's linear blow without stepping out of range. Slipping can be accomplished by quickly snapping the head and upper torso sideways

Tough Enough

(right or left) to avoid the blow.

   snap back—A defensive maneuver that permits you to avoid an assailant's linear and circular blows without stepping out of range. The snap back can be accomplished by quickly snapping the head backward to avoid the assailant's blow.

   somatotypes—A method of classifying human body types or builds into three different categories: endomorph, mesomorph, and ectomorph. See endomorph, mesomorph, and ectomorph.

   sparring—A training exercise where two or more fighters fight each other while wearing protective equipment.

   speed—A physical attribute of armed and unarmed combat. The rate or a measure of the rapid rate of motion.

   spiritual component—One of the three vital components of the CFA system. The spiritual component includes the metaphysical issues and aspects of existence. See physical component and mental component.

   sport-oriented training—Training that is geared for competition and governed by a set of rules. See combat-oriented training and ritual-oriented training.

   sprawling—A grappling technique used to counter a double- or single-leg takedown.

   square off—To be face-to-face with a hostile or threatening assailant who is about to attack you.

   stance—One of the many strategic postures you assume prior to or during armed or unarmed combat.

   stick fighting—Fighting that takes place with either one or two sticks.

   strategic positioning—Tactically positioning yourself to either escape, move behind a barrier, or use a makeshift weapon.

Glossary

strategic/tactical development—One of the five elements of CFA's mental component.

strategy—A carefully planned method of achieving your goal of engaging an assailant under advantageous conditions.

street fight—A spontaneous and violent confrontation between two or more individuals wherein no rules apply.

street fighter—An unorthodox combatant who has no formal training. His combative skills and tactics are usually developed in the street by the process of trial and error.

street training—A CFA training methodology requiring the practitioner to deliver explosive compound attacks for 10 to 20 seconds. See condition ng training and proficiency training.

strength training—The process of developing muscular strength through systematic application of progressive resistance.

striking art—A combat art that relies predominantly on striking techniques to neutralize or terminate a criminal attacker.

striking shield—A rectangular shield constructed of foam and vinyl used to develop power in your kicks, punches, and strikes.

striking tool—A natural body weapon that impacts with the assailant's anatomical target.

strong side—The strongest and most coordinated side of your body.

structure—A definite and organized pattern.

style—The distinct manner in which a fighter executes or performs his combat skills.

stylistic integration—The purposeful and scientific collection of tools and techniques from various disciplines, which are strategically integrated and dramatically altered to meet three essential criteria: efficiency, effectiveness, and combative safety.

submission holds—Also known as control and restraint techniques, many of these locks and holds create sufficient pain to cause the adversary to submit.

system—The unification of principles, philosophies, rules, strategies, methodologies, tools, and techniques of a particular method of combat.

T

tactic—The skill of using the available means to achieve an end.

target awareness—A combative attribute that encompasses five strategic principles: target orientation, target recognition, target selection, target impaction, and target exploitation.

target exploitation—A combative attribute. The strategic maximization of your assailant's reaction dynamics during a fight. Target exploitation can be applied in both armed and unarmed encounters.

target impaction—The successful striking of the appropriate anatomical target.

target orientation—A combative attribute. Having a workable knowledge of the assailant's anatomical targets.

target recognition—The ability to immediately recognize appropriate anatomical targets during an emergency self-defense situation.

target selection—The process of mentally selecting the appropriate anatomical target for your self-defense situation. This is predicated on certain factors, including proper force response, assailant's positioning, and range.

target stare—A form of telegraphing in which you stare at the anatomical target you intend to strike.

Glossary

target zones—The three areas in which an assailant's anatomical targets are located. (See zone one, zone two and zone three.)

technique—A systematic procedure by which a task is accomplished.

telegraphic cognizance—A combative attribute. The ability to recognize both verbal and non-verbal signs of aggression or assault.

telegraphing—Unintentionally making your intentions known to your adversary.

tempo—The speed or rate at which you speak.

terminate—To kill.

terror—The third stage of fear; defined as overpowering fear. See fright and panic.

timing—A physical and mental attribute of armed and unarmed combat. Your ability to execute a movement at the optimum moment.

tone—The overall quality or character of your voice.

tool—See body weapon.

traditional martial arts—Any martial art that fails to evolve and change to meet the demands and characteristics of its present environment.

traditional style/system—See traditional martial arts.

training drills—The various exercises and drills aimed at perfecting combat skills, attributes, and tactics.

trap and tuck - A counter move technique used when the adversary attempts to raze you during your quarter beat assault.

U

unified mind—A mind free and clear of distractions and focused on the combative situation.

use of force response—A combative attribute. Selecting the appropriate level of force for a particular emergency self-defense situation.

V

viciousness—A combative attribute. The propensity to be extremely violent and destructive often characterized by intense savagery.

violence—The intentional utilization of physical force to coerce, injure, cripple, or kill.

visualization—Also known as mental visualization or mental imagery. The purposeful formation of mental images and scenarios in the mind's eye.

W

warm-up—A series of mild exercises, stretches, and movements designed to prepare you for more intense exercise.

weak side—The weaker and more uncoordinated side of your body.

weapon and technique mastery—A component of CFA's physical component. The kinesthetic and psychomotor development of a weapon or combative technique.

weapon capability—An assailant's ability to use and attack with a particular weapon.

webbing - The first phase of the Widow Maker Program. Webbing is a two hand strike delivered to the assailant's chin. It is called Webbing because your hands resemble a large web that wraps around the enemy's face.

widow maker – One who makes widows by destroying husbands.

widow maker program – A CFA combat program specifically designed to teach the law abiding citizen how to use extreme force when faced with immediate threat of unlawful deadly criminal attack. The Widow Maker program is divided into two phases or methodologies: Webbing and Razing.

Y

yell—A loud and aggressive scream or shout used for various strategic reasons.

Z

zero beat – One of the four beat classifications of the Widow Maker, Feral Fighting and Savage Street Fighting Programs. Zero beat strikes are full pressure techniques applied to a specific target until it completely ruptures. They include gouging, crushing, biting, and choking techniques.

zone one—Anatomical targets related to your senses, including the eyes, temple, nose, chin, and back of neck.

zone three—Anatomical targets related to your mobility, including thighs, knees, shins, and instep.

zone two—Anatomical targets related to your breathing, including front of neck, solar plexus, ribs, and groin.

Tough Enough

About Sammy Franco

With over 30 years of experience, Sammy Franco is one of the world's foremost authorities on fighting. Highly regarded as a leading innovator in combat sciences, Mr. Franco was one of the premier pioneers in the field of combat instruction.

Sammy Franco is perhaps best known as the founder and creator of Contemporary Fighting Arts (CFA), a state-of-the-art offensive-based combat system that is specifically designed for real-world self-defense. CFA is a sophisticated and practical system of self-defense, designed specifically to provide efficient and effective methods to avoid, defuse, confront, and neutralize both armed and unarmed attackers.

Sammy Franco has frequently been featured in martial art magazines, newspapers, and appeared on numerous radio and television programs. Mr. Franco has also authored numerous books, magazine articles, and editorials, and has developed a popular library of instructional videos.

Sammy Franco's experience and credibility in the combat sciences is unequaled. One of his many accomplishments in this field includes the fact that he has earned the ranking of a Law Enforcement Master Instructor, and has designed, implemented, and taught officer survival training to the United States Border Patrol (USBP). He has instructed members of the US Secret Service, Military Special Forces, Washington DC Police Department, Montgomery County, Maryland Deputy Sheriffs, and the US Library of Congress Police. Sammy

Tough Enough

Franco is also a member of the prestigious International Law Enforcement Educators and Trainers Association (ILEETA) as well as the American Society of Law Enforcement Trainers (ASLET) and he is listed in the "Who's Who Director of Law Enforcement Instructors."

Sammy Franco is a nationally certified Law Enforcement Instructor in the following curricula: PR-24 Side-Handle Baton, Police Arrest and Control Procedures, Police Personal Weapons Tactics, Police Power Handcuffing Methods, Police Oleoresin Capsicum Aerosol Training (OCAT), Police Weapon Retention and Disarming Methods, Police Edged Weapon Countermeasures and "Use of Force" Assessment and Response Methods.

Mr. Franco holds a Bachelor of Arts degree in Criminal Justice from the University of Maryland. He is a regularly featured speaker at a number of professional conferences and conducts dynamic and enlightening seminars on numerous aspects of self-defense and combat training.

On a personal level, Sammy Franco is an animal lover, who will go to great lengths to assist and rescue animals. Throughout the years, he's rescued everything from turkey vultures to goats. However, his most treasured moments are always spent with his beloved German Shepherd dogs.

For more information about Mr. Franco and his unique Contemporary Fighting Arts system, you can visit his website at: **ContemporaryFightingArts.com** or follow him on twitter @ **RealSammyFranco**

Other Books by Sammy Franco

SPEED BOXING SECRETS
A 21-Day Program to Hitting Faster and Reacting Quicker in Boxing and Mixed Martial Arts
by Sammy Franco

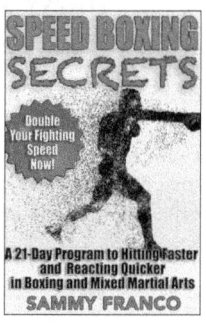

Speed Boxing Secrets: A 21-Day Program to Hitting Faster and Reacting Quicker in Boxing and Mixed Martial Arts is a comprehensive speed acceleration program made for anyone who wants to dramatically improve their fighting speed in a short period of time. When used correctly, this simple speed development program will double your boxing speed in as little as 21 days. 8.5 x 5.5, paperback, photos, illus, 150 pages.

HEAVY BAG TRAINING
For Boxing, Mixed Martial Arts and Self-Defense
(Heavy Bag Training Series Book 1)
by Sammy Franco

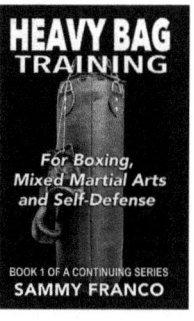

The heavy bag is one of the oldest and most recognizable pieces of training equipment. It's used by boxers, mixed martial artists, self-defense practitioners, and fitness enthusiasts. Unfortunately, most people don't know how to use the heavy bag correctly. Heavy Bag Training teaches you everything you ever wanted to know about working out on the heavy bag. In this one-of-a-kind book, world-renowned self-defense expert Sammy Franco provides you with the knowledge, skills, and attitude necessary to maximize the training benefits of the bag. 8.5 x 5.5, paperback, photos, illus, 172 pages.

HEAVY BAG COMBINATIONS
The Ultimate Guide to Heavy Bag Punching Combinations
(Heavy Bag Training Series Book 2)
by Sammy Franco

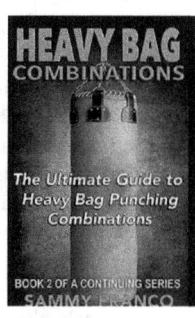

Heavy Bag Combinations is the second book in Sammy Franco's best-selling Heavy Bag Training Series. This unique book is your ultimate guide to mastering devastating heavy bag punching combinations. With over 300+ photographs and detailed step-by-step instructions, Heavy Bag Combinations provides beginner, intermediate and advanced heavy bag workout combinations that will challenge you for the rest of your life! In fact, even the most experienced athlete will advance his fighting skills to the next level and beyond. 8.5 x 5.5, paperback, photos, illus, 248 pages.

HEAVY BAG WORKOUTS
A Hard-Core Guide to Heavy Bag Workout Routines
(Heavy Bag Training Series Book 3)
by Sammy Franco

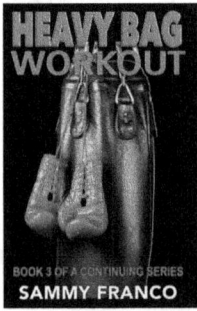

Heavy Bag Workout is the third book in Sammy Franco's best-selling Heavy Bag Training Series. This unique book features over two dozen "out of the box" heavy bag workout routines that will maximize your fighting skills for boxing, mixed martial arts, kick boxing, self-defense, and personal fitness. 8.5 x 5.5, paperback, photos, illus, 208 pages.

HEAVY BAG BIBLE
3 Best-Selling Heavy Bag Books In One Massive Collection
(Heavy Bag Training Series Books 1, 2, 3)
by Sammy Franco

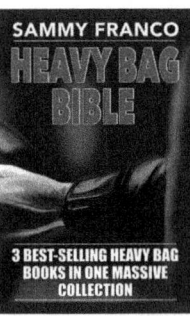

In this unprecedented book collection, world-renowned martial arts and self-defense expert, Sammy Franco takes his thirty years of teaching experience and gives you the most authoritative information for mastering the heavy bag. The Heavy Bag Bible includes Franco's three best-selling heavy bag books collected into one huge paperback collection. This massive 530+ page book contains the entire Heavy Bag Training Series, books 1-3. 8.5 x 5.5, paperback, photos, illus, 538 pages.

DOUBLE END BAG WORKOUT
For Boxing, Mixed Martial Arts & Self-Defense
by Sammy Franco

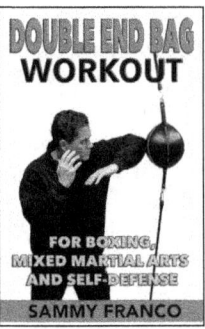

With over 200 detailed photographs, clear illustrations, and easy-to-follow instructions, Double End Bag Workout: For Boxing, Mixed Martial Arts and Self-Defense has everything you need to start training immediately. Double End Bag Workout also has beginner, intermediate and advanced workout routines that improve your speed, timing, accuracy, attack rhythm, and endurance. Whether you're an elite fighter or a complete beginner, this comprehensive book will take your boxing workout to the next level and beyond! 8.5 x 5.5, paperback, photos, illus, 260 pages.

THE COMPLETE BODY OPPONENT BAG BOOK
by Sammy Franco

In this one-of-a-kind book, Sammy Franco teaches you the many hidden training features of the body opponent bag that will improve your fighting skills and boost your conditioning. With detailed photographs, step-by-step instructions, and dozens of unique workout routines, The Complete Body Opponent Bag Book is the authoritative resource for mastering this lifelike punching bag. It covers stances, punching, kicking, grappling techniques, mobility and footwork, targets, fighting ranges, training gear, time based workouts, punching and kicking combinations, weapons training, grappling drills, ground fighting, and dozens of workouts. 8.5 x 5.5, paperback, 139 photos, illustrations, 206 pages.

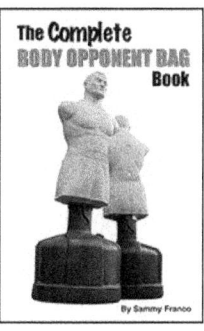

KNOCKOUT
The Ultimate Guide to Sucker Punching
by Sammy Franco

Knockout is a one-of-a-kind book designed to teach you the lost art and science of sucker punching for real-world self-defense situations. With over 150 detailed photographs, 244 pages and dozens of easy-to-follow instructions, Knockout has everything you need to master the devastating art of sucker punching. Whether you are a beginner or advanced, student or teacher, Knockout teaches you brutally effective skills, battle-tested techniques, and proven strategies to get you home alive and in one piece. 8.5 x 5.5, paperback, 244 pages.

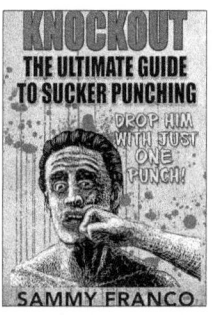

MAXIMUM DAMAGE
Hidden Secrets Behind Brutal Fighting Combination
by Sammy Franco

Maximum Damage teaches you the quickest ways to beat your opponent in the street by exploiting his physical and psychological reactions in a fight. Learn how to stay two steps ahead of your adversary by knowing exactly how he will react to your strikes before they are delivered. In this unique book, reality based self-defense expert Sammy Franco reveals his unique Probable Reaction Dynamic (PRD) fighting method. Probable reaction dynamics are both a scientific and comprehensive offensive strategy based on the positional theory of combat. Regardless of your style of fighting, PRD training will help you overpower your opponent by seamlessly integrating your strikes into brutal fighting combinations that are fast, ferocious and final! 8.5 x 5.5, paperback, 240 photos, illustrations, 238 pages.

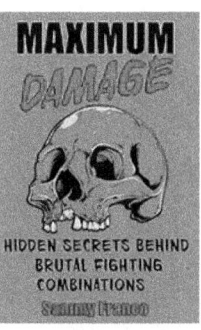

FIRST STRIKE
End a Fight in Ten Seconds or Less!
by Sammy Franco

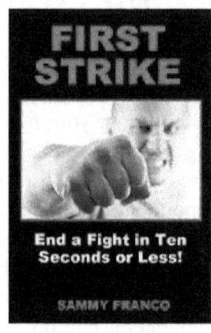

Learn how to stop any attack before it starts by mastering the art of the preemptive strike. First Strike gives you an easy-to-learn yet highly effective self-defense game plan for handling violent close-quarter combat encounters. First Strike will teach you instinctive, practical and realistic self-defense techniques that will drop any criminal attacker to the floor with one punishing blow. By reading this book and by practicing, you will learn the hard-hitting skills necessary to execute a punishing first strike and ultimately prevail in a self-defense situation. 8.5 x 5.5, paperback, photos, illustrations, 202 pages.

THE BIGGER THEY ARE, THE HARDER THEY FALL
How to Fight a Bigger and Stronger Opponent
by Sammy Franco

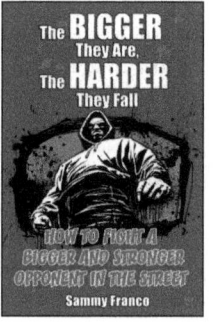

Sammy Franco was concerned that no book on the market successfully tackled the specific problem of fighting a larger, stronger opponent. In The Bigger They Are, The Harder They Fall, he addresses that all-important issue and delivers the solid information you'll need to win a street fight when the odds seem stacked against you. In this one-of-a-kind book, Sammy Franco prepares you both mentally and physically for the fight of your life. Unless you're a lineman for the NFL, there may come a day when you will face an opponent who can dominate you through sheer mass and power. Read and study this book before that day comes. 8.5 x 5.5, paperback, photos, illus, 212 pages.

CONTEMPORARY FIGHTING ARTS, LLC
"Real World Self-Defense Since 1989"
www.SammyFranco.com

www.ingramcontent.com/pod-product-compliance
Lightning Source LLC
Chambersburg PA
CBHW061645040426
42446CB00010B/1584